Wisconsin Harbor Towns

The Ultimate Wisconsin Road Trip

Lori Helke

Next Voyage Press

Copyright © 2024 by Lori Helke

All rights reserved.

No portion of this book may be reproduced in any form without written permission from the publisher or author, except as permitted by U.S. copyright law.

For Megan

"The world is a book, and those who do not travel only read a page." – St. Augustine

Contents

Introduction	1
Wisconsin Harbor Towns Map	6
Kenosha	7
Racine	27
Milwaukee	41
Port Washington	63
Photos Kenosha-Port Washington	74
Sheboygan	75
Manitowoc	95
Two Rivers	113
Photos Sheboygan-Two Rivers	123
Kewaunee	125
Algoma	133
Sturgeon Bay	145
Door County	161
Photos Algoma-DoorCounty	180

Washington Island	181
Green Bay	197
Oconto	215
Marinette	225
Photos Green Bay-Marinette	241
Ashland	243
Washburn	257
Bayfield	267
Superior	283
Photos Ashland-Superior	294
Photo Reference	295

INTRODUCTION

The idea for a Wisconsin Harbor Towns travel guide began in the summer of 2021. I dedicated the previous three years to writing, publishing, and marketing my two children's books, and was ready to try something new. I decided on a book that would unite two of my primary interests: solo midlife travel, and promoting my home state of Wisconsin.

Even in this digital age, when I travel, I rely on book form travel guides. Having all the needed information in a neat package I can study, highlight, and keep in my travel bag is perfect for this traveler. Call me old-fashioned, but I still love books. Plus, the travel writer in me often consults well-worn travel guides when writing blog posts about a trip.

I have lived my entire life (61 years, thank you very much) in Wisconsin. Growing up, we took ALL our family vacations in Wisconsin. As an adult, my husband, Rick, and I have taken a lot of weekend road trips: fishing, snowmobiling, and exploring all over Wisconsin. Today, I am usually on my own (Rick no longer travels) and beachside cities and towns are my favorite destinations to camp and explore.

Which comes back to the reasoning behind this guide. Living near Lake Michigan and having frequent access to all the lakeshore cities prompted me to toy with the concept of the ultimate Wisconsin road trip guide of these increasingly popular harbor towns. Using these lakeside communities as a common denominator for a travel guide was appealing to me.

And so three years later and countless miles put on my car, I accomplished what I set out to do.

About This Guide

I divide each of the 19 Wisconsin Harbor Towns into chapters beginning with the southernmost city Kenosha, then follow the Lake Michigan shoreline north. Then we go on to the four harbor towns on Lake Superior, ending at the city of Superior. Travelers can use this guide for one big road trip, going from harbor town to harbor town. Or divide the guide up into several bucket list road trips, ticking them off as you go along. For example, I recommend touring all four cities on Lake Superior by taking a week or two and spending a few days at each, with perhaps one day spent in Washburn. Ashland, Washburn, and Bayfield are close to each other so you could stay at one and go back and forth and then go to Superior and stay there for a couple of days.

In each chapter, I give a brief introduction and overview of the city with some interesting historical facts. There are things that will appeal to the adult solo traveler, couples, girlfriend getaways, and retirees. This is probably not a guide for families with young children.

At each destination, I focus on:

The **highlights** of each harbor town. I list lighthouses and if they are open to the public, and major attractions, with some lesser known places to go sprinkled in. I also highlight recreational opportunities I've done myself, like kayaking the river in Milwaukee.

If you're looking for shopping, I list interesting places to shop, highlighting unique businesses and sometimes whole shopping districts.

Next, I list some of the **best places to eat and drink**. Cafes, bakeries, restaurants, breweries, wineries, fun bars, and great places to satisfy your sweet tooth are all included.

Finally, I list **accommodations, including hotels**, bed-and-breakfast inns, motels, and campgrounds. Most times I leave out the chain hotels, opting to suggest accommodations that offer a unique experience.

The vast majority of places I list are small businesses. Since Covid in 2020, I have gained a heightened appreciation for them. As I traveled around Wisconsin in research for this book, the sense of community pride in each small business owner I talked to was a common denominator in every city I visited. So please continue to support small businesses. Sometimes that means packing our patience, since many businesses are short-staffed or have limited hours. Be sure and check websites, or call for updated hours.

The road to writing my first travel guide was rocky. It took time to find my groove. I had doubts. I got in my own way many times. But as I visited these harbor towns, I kept a diary and made notes about things that really captured my attention, as well as stories heard while chatting with business owners. It was a fun and motivating experience to meet the people and hear the stories of these Wisconsin Harbor Towns.

And finally, I have an entire community of people and tourism boards to thank for helping me along the way. When I first reached out to them with this project idea, the response was overwhelmingly positive.

First, I could not have pursued this project had it not been for my ongoing relationship with Visit Sheboygan. Not only am I a proud member of its board of directors, but I am thankful for the support and guidance the Visit Sheboygan staff have given me. Special thanks to Janet DeVore, who gave me guidance, and my wonderful friend, Shelly Harms. She has been behind me every step of the way on this project.

I also have to thank the other tourism boards I worked with or hosted me during my visits.

Visit Kenosha

Visit Racine County

Visit Milwaukee

Manitowoc Area Visitors and Convention Bureau

Destination Door County

Visit Oconto County

Explore Marinette County

Ashland Area Chamber Of Commerce

Bayfield and The Apostle Islands

I have to thank my editor, Erin Davisson. She took time out of her busy retirement schedule to be my editor. Not only is she a wonderful editor, but an even more wonderful friend.

Much thanks as well to my friend Theresa Goodrich for all the inspiration, advice, and mentorship.

To my dear friend Barbara Techel. My author journey would not have been possible without her encouragement from the very beginning. It all began with her doing an oracle card reading for me in early 2019. Barb, I may have not written that memoir yet, but I intend to some day.

Finally, I want to thank my family. Rick, for being a tireless supporter of my travel habit and for letting me soar at this later stage of life. My daughter- and son-in-law, Megan and Justin, for their love and support.

And a big shout-out to all the followers of my blog, and social media channels. You are all the best.

Lastly, dear reader, if you enjoy this book and find value in it, please leave a review on Amazon. Thank you so much in advance.

Wisconsin Harbor Towns Map

Kenosha

Our first Wisconsin Harbor Town is Kenosha. The city provides the perfect introduction and sets the tone for all the coastal cities we will explore in this travel guide. Like all our Wisconsin Harbor Towns, Kenosha's focus is its beautiful shoreline, with its expansive green space and centrally-located cultural offerings. Once a booming industrial city, it has become a destination with many wonderful museums, fantastic eateries, and a revitalized downtown area. Whether you're drawn by the allure of historic lighthouses standing guard over azure waves, intrigued by the tales of a town pivotal in the American auto industry, or simply seeking a tranquil escape with scenic beauty at every turn, Kenosha is a destination where every visit feels like a discovery.

What I enjoy about Kenosha is its unexpected treasures and many museums. Kenosha is a budget-friendly destination, with many free museums and dining options that won't break the bank.

The incredible staff at **Visit Kenosha** are a valuable and up-to-date resource for everything Kenosha. To go more in depth, visit their website.

600 52nd Street, Suite 140

visitkenosha.com

Location

Kenosha is located a bit over six miles north of the Wisconsin/ Illinois state line. The scenic route takes you up Highway 32 along Lake Michigan, or the faster way is taking I-94. Downtown Kenosha is approximately seven miles east of the interstate, in some places the city line butts up to the interstate.

Kenosha Facts

- **Kenosha's key role in the American Auto Industry:** Kenosha stakes its claim as a pivotal city in the American auto industry's history, beginning in 1902 with the birth of the Rambler. Thomas Jeffery's Rambler was the second mass-produced auto manufactured in the United States. In 1916, Charles Nash bought the company for 5 million and changed its name to Nash Motors Company. This company was innovative in its approach to automobile design and manufacturing, setting standards that would influence the industry for years to come. Kenosha also played a role in workers' rights, eventually unionizing in 1933, two years before joining the newly formed United Auto Workers union in 1935. The city's auto legacy continued with American Motors Corporation (AMC) until Chrysler stopped its automobile production in the late 1980s, marking the end of an era for Kenosha as a hub of automobile production. Automobile engine production continued until 2010.

- **A Cultural Hub with Immigrant Roots:** Waves of immigrants have profoundly shaped Kenosha's cultural landscape, beginning with Yankee and European settlers in the 1830s. These diverse communities brought with them their traditions, crafts, and culinary heritage, contributing to the rich mosaic of Kenosha's culture today.

- **Kenosha is home to many well-known companies:** Today a variety of well-known companies make Kenosha home. Among them is Snap-On, Inc., Jockey International, Inc., Ocean Spray, and Uline. Amazon operates a distribution center in Kenosha and Haribo's first North American manufacturing plant makes its sweet treats here.

- **Kenosha's relationship to Chicago:** Even though Milwaukee is closer than Chicago, Kenosha is considered a "satellite city" to Chicago. To my absolute joy, the Chicago suburban Metra train makes Kenosha its northernmost stop. It's my favorite mode of transportation to Chicago, because it's stress-free and budget friendly.

- **Population:** The population of Kenosha is 98,484 (2022).

How Much Time To Spend In Kenosha

I love to add on a day or two visit to Kenosha and then combine that with an overnight visit to Chicago. Kenosha is worthy of a full weekend of exploring, even more if you want to really appreciate the vibe of the city.

Things To Do In Kenosha

Kenosha Highlights

Lighthouses

Both of Kenosha's historic lighthouses are located on Simmons Island.

North Pier Lighthouse- The Kenosha North Pier Lighthouse, an active navigation aid, stands as a testament to Kenosha's maritime history. Established in the early 20th century, this lighthouse replaced Southport Lighthouse, embodying the technological advancements of its time. Its strategic position on the north pier of Kenosha's harbor has guided countless vessels through the waters of Lake

Michigan, ensuring their safe passage to and from Kenosha's shores. It is listed on the National Register of Historic Places.

While the lighthouse itself is not open for public tours and is privately owned, visitors can walk along the pier to get a closer look at this historic red structure.

The walk to the lighthouse offers breathtaking views of Lake Michigan and the Kenosha shoreline, making it a popular spot for photographers, sunrise watchers, and those simply enjoying the beauty of the lakefront. Practice caution when walking out to the lighthouse since bad weather can make the walk unsafe.

End of 50th Street

.visitkenosha.com/things-to-do/attractions/lighthouses

Southport Lighthouse and Museum- The Southport Light Station Museum includes the historic **Southport Lighthouse** and the adjacent Lighthouse Keeper's House. The lighthouse was first lit in 1866, serving as a critical beacon for ships navigating the treacherous waters of Lake Michigan. The Lighthouse Keeper's House, built in the same period, has been meticulously restored to its 19th-century appearance, offering a glimpse into the life of a lighthouse keeper and his family.

The Southport Light Station Museum invites visitors to explore its rich history, with the option of climbing the 72 step spiral staircase up the lighthouse tower for a panoramic view of Lake Michigan and the surrounding area. The museum, in the Lighthouse Keeper's House, features exhibits on maritime history, the development of Kenosha's harbor, and the evolution of lighthouse technology. It is open May through October and is a required visit for those interested in lighthouses and maritime and Kenosha history.

5117 4th Avenue

kenoshahistorycenter.org/lightstation.html

Kenosha History Center

For those interested in Kenosha's history, visit the Kenosha History Center either before or after your visit to the Southport Lighthouse and Museum. Inside you'll find exhibits that celebrate Kenosha's automobile history and other businesses, a display telling the history of Kenosha, a gift shop, and the Kenosha Historical Society archives.

220 51st Place

kenoshahistorycenter.org/geninfo.html

HarborPark

HarborPark is a beautifully developed area that wraps around Kenosha's Lake Michigan shoreline, offering a mix of natural beauty, recreational facilities, and cultural attractions. It's a place where history, art, and leisure converge against the backdrop of stunning lake views. Key features include meticulously landscaped gardens, walkable promenades, and the captivating Kenosha Sculpture Walk, which showcases an array of intriguing artworks along the lakefront.

Civil War Museum

The Civil War Museum focuses on the Civil War from the perspective of the Upper Midwest, offering a unique angle on the conflict that shaped America. Through immersive exhibits and artifacts, it explores the personal stories of soldiers, civilians, and freedmen, providing insights into how the war impacted the region and its people.

The museum features a 360-degree film, "Seeing the Elephant," which offers a first-person experience of a soldier's life during the Civil War, providing an immersive glimpse into history. This film is well worth the admission to see it. Visitors will appreciate the museum's thoughtful approach to storytelling, its educational programs, and the depth of its collections. It's a poignant reminder of the impact of the Civil War on the Midwest and the nation. General admission to the museum is free, but there is a fee for The Fiery Trial exhibit and admission to the film.

5400 1st Avenue

museums.kenosha.org/civil-war-museum

Kenosha Public Museum

The Kenosha Public Museum is a natural sciences and fine arts museum, home to over 80,000 pieces, including mammoth bones found in the area, Native American artifacts, and fine art collections. Its exhibits range from geological specimens to contemporary art, making it a diverse and engaging cultural space.

The museum's "Mammoths at the Museum" exhibit displays a nearly complete replica of the wooly mammoth skeleton which was unearthed locally, highlighting Kenosha's significance in paleontological research. There is a fascinating timeline and replica of each archeological dig site. It's hard to believe that of the 26 known mammoth sites in the United States, two are in Kenosha, the rest are in the western part of the country.

The museum offers an array of exhibits that cater to diverse interests, from history buffs to art lovers wanting to explore the natural and cultural heritage of the region.

Admission is free for all visitors, making it an accessible educational experience for everyone. (Photo page 74)

5500 1st Avenue

museums.kenosha.org

Dinosaur Discovery Museum

This museum is the only one dedicated to the exploration of the link between birds and dinosaurs, showcasing one of the most significant collections of meat-eating dinosaurs in the country. Its interactive exhibits and educational programs make it an engaging experience for visitors of all ages.

5608 10th Avenue

museums.kenosha.org/dinosaur-discovery-museum

Kenosha Streetcars

This is one of Kenosha's most beloved gems. Riding the electric Kenosha Streetcars is like stepping back in time. It's an affordable, fun, and convenient way to see the city, highlighting Kenosha's commitment to preserving its historical heritage while serving the needs of modern residents and visitors. The two-mile loop connects various points of interest, including parks, museums, the Metra train station and shopping districts, making it an essential Kenosha experience. The fare is just one dollar, with an all-day pass costing $3.50. Streetcars contain a lift, making them wheelchair accessible.

724 54th Street

.visitkenosha.com/listing/electric-streetcar/268/

Kenosha HarborMarket

Located outdoors during the warmer months and indoors in the winter, the Kenosha HarborMarket is a vibrant Saturday marketplace featuring local artisans, farmers, and chefs. It offers fresh produce, gourmet foods, crafts, and live entertainment, creating a lively community gathering space.

Summer Market: 2nd Avenue between 54th and 56th Streets

Winter Market: 3030 39th Avenue

kenoshaharbormarket.com

Petrifying Springs Park

As Kenosha County's oldest park, Petrifying Springs Park offers an abundance of natural beauty across its 360 acres. It features picturesque hiking trails about three to five miles in length, plus beginner and intermediate mountain biking trails, a challenging 18-hole golf course, and picnic areas amidst rolling hills and mature forests. Your furry friends can run around in the dog park. There's even a biergarten in the park.

5555 7th Street

kenoshacounty.org/1652/Petrifying-Springs-Park

Simmons Island

Kenosha has five beaches to explore, but my favorite is on Simmons Island. I wrote about it earlier since it's home to both lighthouses, but there's so much more on the island. You can find a park, boardwalk, and a playground. On the island, you can rent kayaks and paddleboards, and also take sailing lessons with the Kenosha Community Sailing Center. The beach is accessible to all with the addition of special beach mats in the summer. With easy access to downtown, you can easily spend a whole day here.

visitkenosha.com/listing/simmons-island-park-and-beach/372/

Other beaches in Kenosha are at:

Alford Park

Eichelman Park

Pennoyer Park

Southport Park

Hawthorn Hollow Nature Sanctuary and Arboretum

This nature sanctuary and arboretum offer a peaceful retreat with beautiful gardens, hiking trails, and a collection of historic buildings that showcase Wisconsin's natural and cultural history. It's a perfect place for nature lovers to explore diverse ecosystems, enjoy bird watching, or learn about environmental conservation and local history. Admission is free.

880 Green Bay Road

hawthornhollow.org

Bristol Renaissance Faire

Perhaps one of the best known things to do in Kenosha is time traveling back to medieval England. The Bristol Renaissance Faire draws crowds every summer from all over. It's huge (over 30 acres) and whether or not you come in costume, you will carry around a turkey leg at some point. Open July through Labor Day weekend.

renfair.com/bristol

Shopping

Mars Cheese Castle

No visit to Kenosha is complete without a stop at Mars Cheese Castle, a landmark destination that has been celebrating Wisconsin's cheese heritage for decades. This iconic store features an extensive selection of cheeses, meats, and local specialties, along with a bakery and deli. Have the fried cheese curds because you just have to.

2800 West frontage Road

.marscheese.com/index.html

Blue House Books

Blue House Books is a charming, independent bookstore that prides itself on fostering a love for reading within the community. The store offers a carefully curated selection of books across various genres, featuring both bestsellers and works by local authors. It also hosts book signings, readings, and community events, making it a hub for literary enthusiasts.

5915 6th Avenue A

blue-house-books.com

Jockey Factory Store

As a brand that originated in Kenosha, Jockey offers a comprehensive retail experience in its hometown factory store. Shoppers can find a wide range of undergarments, activewear, and accessories at competitive prices.

5500 6th Avenue

Tenuta's Deli

A Kenosha staple for 74 years, Tenuta's Deli is much more than a deli—it's an institution. Here you can find an extensive selection of Italian groceries, fine cheeses, meats, and an impressive array of imported and domestic beers and wines.

3203 52nd Street

.tenutasdeli.com

Mike Bjorn's Fine Clothing

A landmark in Kenosha, Mike Bjorn's offers a wide variety of men's formalwear, casual wear, and everything in between. Known for its colorful interior and eclectic selection, it's a go-to destination for those looking to stand out with their wardrobe choices. Even if you're not in the market for a suit, a browse inside this store will be a delight for your eyes.

5614 6th Avenue

mikebjorns.com

Sandy's Popper

Sandy's Popper is a popular local spot for homemade gourmet popcorn and ice cream. With a variety of popcorn flavors made on-site and a selection of classic and unique ice cream flavors, it's a must-visit for those with a sweet tooth.

5700 6th Avenue

sandyspopper.com

Authentique

Authentique is a boutique that specializes in gifts, home decor, and personal items, all with a unique, artisanal touch. It's known for its carefully curated selection that emphasizes quality and individuality.

625 57th Street

authentiquegifts.com

Places to eat and drink in Kenosha

Kenosha has a vibrant dining scene. Its list of incredible options is long. There are dining options for all price points, fun, innovative cuisine, and retro cool places. I've listed a good sampling of suggestions here.

Coffee and Bakery

The Buzz Cafe

Whatever you want to drink, Buzz has it. Coffee, a wide selection of Rishi Tea, beer and wine. You'll find a small breakfast and lunch menu. I like the variety and the downtown location can't be beat.

5621 6th Avenue

.buzzcafekenosha.com

Daily Dose Cafe

Daily Dose Cafe is a vibrant local coffee shop that focuses on creating a positive atmosphere where community members can gather. They offer a variety of coffee drinks, teas, and smoothies, made from high-quality ingredients.

6010 40th Avenue

dailydosecafe.net

Anna's On The Lake

Formerly Common Grounds, this cafe switched owners in 2022. Anna is a Kenosha native who has kept the coffee scene alive in the historic cream city brick building with a fabulous view of the Kenosha Harbor. Anna has a breakfast and lunch menu and the outside bar and grill are open seasonally. If you need a place to stay, there is an upstairs apartment for rent with a wonderful lake view.

5159 6th Avenue

annasonthelakekenosha.com

Paielli's Bakery

Paielli's Bakery is a family-owned establishment that has been serving Kenosha since 1923. Renowned for its traditional Italian breads, rolls, and a wide selection of pastries, Paielli's combines Old World recipes with fresh ingredients to create baked goods adored by locals and visitors alike. From doughnuts to cakes and everything in between, the bakery offers a vast array of choices that cater to every taste.

6020 39th Avenue

paiellisbakery.com

Oliver's Bakery

Oliver's Bakery is another long-time local favorite, known for its creative cakes, cookies, and morning pastries. This bakery prides itself on making all its offerings from scratch, ensuring high-quality treats that are delightful.

3526 Roosevelt Road

oliversbakery.net

Restaurants

Waterfront Warehouse

Waterfront Warehouse is a fantastic addition to Kenosha's dining scene, offering a lunch and dinner menu focused on modern American cuisine with a creative twist. The restaurant's interior features a rustic-industrial decor, providing a cozy yet chic dining atmosphere. It also offers a gluten-free and vegan menu, easy choices for those with dietary needs.

3322 Sheridan Road

eatatww.com/index.php

Sazzy B

Sazzy B is a vibrant spot in the heart of downtown Kenosha that offers an eclectic menu featuring global flavors. With live music on select nights and a stylish, upbeat atmosphere, it's a great place to enjoy everything from gourmet burgers to innovative entrees. My favorite cool element, the menu, suggests wine pairings with each dinner entrée. Sazzy B also has a full brunch menu on the weekends.

5623 6th Avenue

.sazzybhive.com

Boat House Dockside Pub & Eatery

Located directly on the waterfront, The Boat House Pub & Eatery offers stunning views of Lake Michigan, making it a favorite among locals and visitors alike. Known for its seafood and American classics, the restaurant provides a cozy, nautical-themed atmosphere.

4917 7th Avenue

boathousekenosha.com

Frank's Diner

Frank's Diner is a Kenosha landmark and a quintessential American diner known for its generous breakfasts and lunches and great prices. Housed in a classic lunch car diner, it's famous for its "Garbage Plate," a hearty mix of eggs, meats, and vegetables. In my book, Frank's is a required stop.

508 58th Street

franksdinerkenosha.com

The Brat Stop

The Brat Stop is a Wisconsin institution, serving up famous bratwurst, cheese, and other local favorites since 1961. This restaurant and cheese market also features live music and sports viewing areas, making it a popular gathering spot. Definitely another required stop.

12304 75th Street

bratstop.com

Bristol 45 Diner

Let's go west of I94 now with this fun stop. Bristol 45 Diner takes you back in time with its 1950s-themed decor, complete with a jukebox, neon lights, and classic diner fare. This spot offers a variety of American classics, from burgers and shakes to breakfast served all day.

8321 200th Avenue (Highway 45), Bristol

bristol45diner.com

Bars, Wineries, and Breweries

Public Craft Brewing Co.

In the heart of downtown Kenosha, Public Craft Brewing Co. produces an array of quality craft beers. From stouts to IPAs to experimental brews, Public Craft has something to satisfy every beer lover's palate. The taproom offers a cozy, inviting atmosphere where you can sample a rotating selection of craft beers (please try the 'Never A Dill Moment' and get back to me), often accompanied by live music and events. Their commitment to community and quality makes it a local favorite.

628 58th Street

publiccraftbrewing.com

Rustic Road Brewing

Rustic Road Brewing Company is a microbrewery that prides itself on crafting unique, small-batch beers. They offer a creative lineup that includes everything from traditional styles to innovative brews that challenge the palate. The brewery features a comfortable taproom where you can enjoy their beers and often take part in brewery tours and brewing classes. It's a great place to learn about the brewing process while enjoying some fine ales.

5706 6th Avenue

rusticbrewing.com

Sweet Treats

Smarty's Sweets & Treats

Serving up, boba, frappes, Italian sodas, smoothies, and teas, Smarty's is a fun place to check out. I love their selection of freeze-dried candies. Go to the Facebook page for hours.

5821 6th Avenue A

Sweet Corner Ice Cream

Sweet Corner Ice Cream is a beloved local ice cream shop known for its wide array of homemade ice cream flavors. From classic favorites like vanilla and chocolate to inventive creations unique to Sweet Corner, this shop offers something to please every palate. The ice cream is made on-site using high-quality ingredients, ensuring a satisfying experience. Open seasonally.

4919 60th Street

sweetcornericecream.com

Scoops Ice Cream & Candy

A classic ice cream parlor with a twist, Scoops offers a vast array of ice cream flavors along with a full candy bar that includes old-fashioned favorites and new treats.

5711 8th Avenue

scoopskenosha.com

Accommodations

Hotels

There are several budget-friendly hotel chains available in Kenosha and the surrounding area for a comfortable stay in Kenosha.

Apis Hotel & Restaurant

The Apis Hotel and Restaurant is a premiere destination in Kenosha, combining luxury accommodations with exceptional dining in an elegantly designed setting. The hotel provides modern decor, comfortable bedding, and state-of-the-art amenities in each of the six guest rooms and suites. Known for its farm-to-table cuisine, the restaurant at the Apis uses local and seasonal ingredients, including honey from their on-site apiary. For those seeking a refined experience, the Apis Hotel and Restaurant are perfect. The hotel's focus on sustainability and local sourcing is also a significant draw, appealing to eco-conscious travelers.

614 56th Street

attheapis.com

The Stella Hotel & Ballroom

The Stella Hotel & Ballroom is a beautifully restored historic property that brings together classic historic charm with modern amenities. In the heart of downtown Kenosha, this 80 room hotel features elegant guest rooms, a fitness center, and a stunning ballroom that harks back to its origins in 1919. This location has had many lives, beginning with being home to the Pettit Malting Company in 1857, which was destroyed by fire in 1914. The property then housed the former Kenosha Elks Club, the Heritage House Inn, and finally The Stella. The hotel also has an on-site cafe and a restaurant.

5706 8th Avenue

stellahotel.com

The Coffee Pot Inn

The Coffee Pot Inn is above the beloved **Coffee Pot Diner,** another iconic coffee spot, which offers an upper flat that can accommodate six people. There are three bedrooms, a full kitchen, one bathroom, family room, and an enclosed sunroom decorated with the retro-chic flair that matches the diner's ambiance.

4914 7th Avenue

coffeepotkenosha.com

Campgrounds

Richard Bong State Recreation Area

I touch on Richard Bong in the Superior chapter, who was a retired American fighter pilot, famous for his service during World War II. This abandoned jet fighter base is named after him. Even though the base was never built, a group of local citizens protected the site and turned it into this popular area for outdoor recreation. There are hiking and biking trails, a nature center, lookout tower, opportunities for fishing, and more. The campground comprises 217 sites, 54 with electric hookups (most in the Sunrise Campground), and accessible sites. There are six group campsite areas. You'll find a shower building, flush and vault toilets, a dump station, and an accessible cabin for those with disabilities. A Wisconsin State Park sticker is required.

26313 Burlington Road, Kansasville

dnr.wisconsin.gov/topic/parks/richardbong/recreation/camping

Racine

Embark on a journey to Racine, a vibrant jewel on the shores of Lake Michigan, and discover why this harbor town is a pivotal stop on your Wisconsin Harbor Towns road trip.

Racine is famous for being the home of that famous Danish, the oval pastry known as the kringle (Wisconsin's Official State Pastry). Besides that distinction, Racine also has an array of attractions that appeal equally to art lovers, history enthusiasts, and outdoor adventurers. The town's commitment to preserving its storied industrial past, while boldly embracing the future, offers a dynamic visit that promises new discoveries with each return. From the architectural masterpieces by Frank Lloyd Wright to the bustling marina and picturesque North Beach, every corner of Racine invites visitors to partake of its many layers, just like the 32 fine layers that make up that famous kringle.

Racine is bound to surprise and enchant you, just as it does me.

For more information about Racine's many treasures, be sure and stop at the Racine County Visitors Center.

14015 Washington Avenue (Highway 20), Sturtevant

visitracinecounty.com

Location

Downtown Racine is about nine miles east of I-94 north of Kenosha and about 25 miles south of Milwaukee. For a more leisurely route, you can take Highway 32 along Lake Michigan.

Racine Facts

- **Inventive Spirit**: Racine is the birthplace of the garbage disposal, invented by architect John W. Hammes in 1927. That paved the way for the InSinkErator Manufacturing Company in 1938, which still operates today.

- **Architectural Gem:** The city is home to several Frank Lloyd Wright-designed buildings, including the SC Johnson Administration Building and Wingspread, highlighting its rich architectural heritage.

- **Roots in Manufacturing**: Once a leading manufacturer of farm machinery, Racine was home to one of the industry's pioneers, Jerome I. Case. Malted milk was also produced in Racine, by brothers James and William Horlick. Racine's industrial prowess contributed significantly to its growth and development.

- **Cultural Hub:** Racine's vibrant arts scene is anchored by the Racine Art Museum (RAM), known for its significant collection of contemporary craft and art.

- **Population:** With a population of approximately 77,432 (as of 2021), Racine is a bustling community that retains a small-town feel, offering a friendly and welcoming atmosphere to all who visit.

How Much Time To Spend

Allow a couple of days to explore Racine. A day is doable to hit some major sites, but I would suggest two or three days.

Things To Do In Racine

Racine Highlights

Lighthouse

Wind Point Lighthouse- One of the tallest and oldest active lighthouses on the Great Lakes, Wind Point Lighthouse offers breathtaking views and a rich history. Visitors can tour the lighthouse and keeper's house during specific dates during the summer, experiencing a piece of maritime history first-hand. If I had to choose, this may be my favorite lighthouse in Wisconsin. (Photo page 74)

4725 Lighthouse Drive

windpointlighthouse.org

Wind Point Lighthouse

Try The Official Pastry Of Wisconsin

Since Racine is famous for the Kringle, you simply must stop at one of the bakeries that specialize in this local treat. This oval shaped, multi-layered, light and flaky pastry can be filled with everything from the classic almond to key lime. The kringle was brought over by Dutch immigrants who settled in the area. There are a number of bakeries where you can find it. My favorite is Larsen Bakery.

Bendtsen's Bakery

3200 Washington Avenue

bendtsensbakery.com

O&H Danish Bakery

Multiple Locations

ohdanishbakery.com

Larsen Bakery

3311 Washington Avenue

larsenbakery.com

North Beach

Racine's North Beach is a beautiful sandy retreat recognized as one of the best beaches in the Midwest. With its clean, soft sand and clear waters, it's a perfect spot for swimming, sunbathing, and volleyball. The beach is also home to Beachside Oasis, offering refreshments and live music during the summer months. With the addition of a Mobi Mat, the beach is accessible for those with disabilities.

100 Kewaunee Street

cityofracine.org/NorthBeach

Sc Johnson Campus

Explore the innovative designs of Frank Lloyd Wright through a tour of the SC Johnson Administration Building and Research Tower. These architectural masterpieces highlight Wright's organic architecture principles and are a must-visit for architecture enthusiasts. You can also tour The Johnson Foundation at **Wingspread** conference center, once the Wright-designed home of Herbert F. Johnson.

SC Johnson Campus

1525 Howe Street

scjohnson.com/en/interacting-with-sc-johnson/tours-and-architecture

Wingspread

33 East 4 Mile Road, Wind Point

reservations.scjohnson.com/Info.aspx?EventID=21

Racine Art Museum

Home to one of North America's largest collections of contemporary crafts, RAM features works in ceramics, fibers, glass, metals, and wood. Its dynamic exhibitions and engaging programs make it a cornerstone of Racine's cultural community.

441 Main Street

ramart.org

Racine Heritage Museum

Delve into local history at the Racine Heritage Museum, where exhibits cover the area's maritime, industrial, and social past. The museum offers a deep dive into how Racine became the city it is today.

701 Main Street

racineheritagemuseum.org

Rent A Kayak At River Bend Nature Center and Paddle The Root River.

For those who love the outdoors, the River Bend Nature Center provides a perfect escape into Racine's natural beauty. This environmental education center spans over 78 acres and offers opportunities for canoeing, hiking, and wildlife observation. Its serene trails and picturesque river views make it an ideal spot for nature lovers of all ages. The center also hosts educational programs and workshops aimed at promoting environmental awareness and conservation.

3600 North Green Bay Road

riverbendracine.org

Quilts On Barns Tour

Experience the unique "Quilts on Barns" tour, showcasing beautifully painted quilt patterns on historic barns throughout Racine County. This driving tour combines art, history, and the scenic countryside.

visitracinecounty.com/things-to-do/quilts-on-barns/

Shopping

Milaeger's

Give yourself an hour at least to explore Milaeger's, a family-owned business known for its extensive selection of home and garden products. From unique plants and gardening supplies to home decor and apparel, Milaeger's offers quality items that cater to both the enthusiastic gardener and the home decorator. On Sundays, you can find a large farmers market here.

4838 Douglas Avenue

milaegers.com

Lornacopia

Lornacopia is a local favorite, offering a mix of new and consignment clothing as well as women's accessories. Sizes run from x-small to size 3x, making this a wonderfully welcoming shop for women of all sizes. The shop has an upscale feel with its large windows. I may have fallen a bit in love with this boutique.

310 6th Street

lornacopia.com

Hot Shop Glass

For a truly immersive shopping experience, visit Hot Shop Glass, where you can watch skilled artisans create glass art right before your eyes. This studio and gallery not only sells beautiful glass pieces but also offers workshops for those interested in learning the craft. I took a glass fusing class here and came home with a beautiful bracelet.

239 Wisconsin Avenue

hotshopglass.com

Places to eat and drink in Racine

Coffee and Bakery

Mocha Lisa Coffeehouse

Cozy up with a cup of coffee or tea at Mocha Lisa Coffeehouse. This inviting cafe inside a converted house boasts a wide selection of beverages, homemade pastries, and light fare, making it the perfect spot for breakfast or a mid-day treat. There is so much to see in this cool place. Mocha Lisa has an extensive collection of local artist's wares here for you to bring home. Simply adorable.

2825 4 ½ Mile Road

mochalisacoffeehouse.com

Wilson's Coffee and Tea

Wilson's Coffee & Tea is Racine's oldest coffee shop and roastery, offering a broad selection of freshly roasted coffees that you can enjoy onsite or take home. The shop prides itself on its community feel and knowledgeable staff who are always ready to help you pick the perfect brew.

3306 Washington Avenue

wilsonscoffee.com

Restaurants

The Maple Table

The Maple Table is known for its exceptional brunch offerings. Featuring locally sourced ingredients, this restaurant offers a fresh take on American classics, with menu highlights including artisanal pancakes, gourmet omelets, and unique brunch cocktails. The Corned Beef Hash was an amazing indulgence.

520 Main Street

themapletable.com

Olde Madrid

Olde Madrid brings the vibrant flavors of Spain to Racine, offering a cozy atmosphere where guests can enjoy authentic tapas, paellas, and a variety of Spanish wines. It's the perfect spot for a romantic dinner or a lively meal with friends.

418 6th Street

oldemadrid.com

Kewpie Sandwich Shop

A Racine staple since 1926, Kewpie Sandwich Shop is beloved for its burgers and homemade root beer at incredible prices. This vintage diner captures the essence of a classic American burger joint, making it a must-visit for both locals and tourists. The fun atmosphere and full display of kewpie dolls add to the charm of this place. Cash only.

520 Wisconsin Avenue

Phone: (262) 634-9601

Salute Italian Restaurant

Salute Italian Restaurant brings the heart and soul of Italian cuisine to Racine. With a menu that celebrates traditional flavors, diners can enjoy a variety of pastas, pizzas, and Italian entrees. The warm ambiance and friendly service make it an excellent choice for a family meal or a romantic dinner.

314 Main Street

saluteitalianracine.com

Asiana Asian Cuisine

Asiana Asian Cuisine Restaurant offers a broad menu, featuring dishes from across the Asian continent, including Chinese, Korean, and Japanese favorites. Known for its sushi rolls and vibrant flavors, Asiana is a go-to for those craving a diverse and delicious Asian dining experience.

423 6th Street

asianaracine.com

Reefpoint Brew House

Located on Racine's waterfront, Reefpoint Brew House is not just a restaurant but also a prime spot for enjoying local and regional craft beers. With a broad selection of brews on tap and a lively atmosphere, it's a favorite among locals for a night out or a casual drink overlooking the water.

2 Christopher Columbus Causeway

reefpointbrewhouse.com

Bars, Wineries, and Breweries

Uncorkt

Uncorkt offers a relaxed, upscale atmosphere where guests can enjoy an extensive selection of wines from around the world. The knowledgeable staff can guide you in choosing the perfect wine to enjoy in the shop or to take home. They also host regular tasting events and wine education classes.

240 Main Street

uncorkt.com

Sweet Treats

Divino Gelato Cafe

I cannot resist gelato no matter where I am and to say I was happy to find this place is an understatement. For a sweet treat with an Italian twist, stop by Divino Gelato Café. They offer a wide range of gelato flavors made from fresh, high-quality ingredients. Whether you prefer classic chocolate or something more exotic like lavender, there's a flavor to satisfy your palate. They also serve another of my favorites, macarons.

245 Main Street

divinogelatocafe.com

Accommodations

Hotels

There are a large number of chain hotels and motels located in and near Racine.

Doubletree by Hilton Racine Harbourwalk

Located along the scenic waterfront, DoubleTree by Hilton offers stunning views of Lake Michigan and comfortable, modern accommodations. Guests enjoy amenities such as an indoor pool, fitness center, and on-site dining, making it a perfect choice for both leisure and business travelers.

223 Gaslight Circle

hilton.com/en/hotels/racgldt-doubletree-racine-harbourwalk

Hotel Verdant

Hotel Verdant offers a blend of modern amenities and eco-friendly design, providing a luxurious yet sustainable stay in the heart of Racine. The hotel features sophisticated rooms with contemporary decor, a state-of-the-art fitness center, and a rooftop lounge that offers spectacular views of the city and Lake Michigan. It's an excellent choice for travelers seeking comfort and style with a minimal environmental footprint.

245 Main Street

hotelverdant.com

Campgrounds

Cliffside Campground

For those who prefer the great outdoors, Cliffside Campground offers both basic and electric hook-up sites. Located atop the bluffs overlooking Lake Michigan, it provides a stunning natural setting with ample opportunities for hiking, bird-watching, and enjoying the peaceful outdoor environment. I really enjoyed camping here and taking the short hike to the cliff with its breathtaking view of the lake. It's easy access to downtown Racine. The rates are not bad, since it's a part of the parks system. There are 92 sites, two shower/restroom facilities, and a dump station. Each site also has water hookup.

7320 Michna Road, Caldonia

Phone: (262) 886-8457

Milwaukee

Milwaukee is Wisconsin's largest city. It's also known as the "City Of Festivals" and "Brew City". First-time visitors are often in awe during their first trip to Milwaukee. They quickly learn that this city is overflowing with wonderful architecture, amazing food, and an art and cultural focus that rivals much larger cities.

As someone who lives just an hour north of Milwaukee, I always took it for granted, usually only visiting when I wanted to go to a concert, or an event like Summerfest. Aren't we often guilty of this, opting to visit faraway places and ignoring what's in front of us? All that changed when I attended a travel conference in Milwaukee a few years ago. Women from all over the United States attended, most visiting Milwaukee for the first time. I had the opportunity to see the city through the eyes of these well-traveled women who were appreciating the architecture, food, and culture of the city. I now visit Milwaukee like a tourist, appreciative of all her charms as well as her grit.

Milwaukee stands out as a vibrant urban hub on the western shore of Lake Michigan. Renowned for its rich brewing heritage, Milwaukee seamlessly blends historical charm with contemporary vibrancy. The city is a tapestry of cultural diversity, offering a wide array of activities ranging from the arts to sports, making it a magnet for tourists and residents alike. Whether you're drawn to explore its celebrated museums, relax in its beautiful parks, or indulge in its varied culinary scene, Milwaukee promises an unforgettable experience filled with warmth, discovery, and entertainment.

Just like Door County, Milwaukee is worthy of its own travel guide, and there are some valuable resources out there. **Visit Milwaukee** is the official tourism entity for Milwaukee and its website and visitor's guide can help.

visitmilwaukee.org

Location

Arrive in Milwaukee via I-94 and I-43, the main interstate highways that run through Milwaukee. From our last Wisconsin Harbor Town, Racine, Milwaukee is about 30 miles north. You can either take I-94 or the more scenic Highway 32 from Racine. I-41 also runs through the city.

City Facts

- The merging of three separate towns (Juneautown, Kilbourntown, and Walker's Point) in the 1830s founded Milwaukee, with each town established by different settlers: Solomon Juneau, Byron Kilbourn, and George H. Walker.

- During the late 19th century, several large breweries, including Pabst, Blatz, Miller, and Schlitz, made Milwaukee the "Beer Capital of the World." These companies played a significant role in Milwaukee's economy and cultural identity.

- Similar to the Great Chicago Fire, Milwaukee experienced a devastating fire in 1892, which destroyed more than 440 buildings in the Third Ward downtown area, prompting new fire safety regulations and rebuilding efforts that shaped the city's development.

- Milwaukee hosts the world's largest music festival, Summerfest, which attracts nearly one million music fans a year.

- As of the latest data, Milwaukee has a population of approximately 563,305 (2022), making it a bustling urban center.

How Much Time To Spend

To truly appreciate Milwaukee's diverse attractions, plan for at least a weekend. Those with a keen interest in museums, breweries, and cultural festivities might wish to extend their visit to a full week.

Things To Do In Milwaukee

Honestly, I am only able to skim the list of highlights in Milwaukee. There are so many things to do. I tried to list some well known things and some lesser known for variety, to give the essence of what Milwaukee is all about.

Milwaukee Highlights

Lighthouses

North Point Lighthouse is an essential stop for anyone visiting Milwaukee, offering a blend of historical enrichment and stunning scenic views. The lighthouse stands inside picturesque Lake Park, one of Frederick Law Olmsted's beautifully designed landscapes. This historic lighthouse has guided ships since 1888 and became fully automated in 1994. Today, it stands not only as a beacon of maritime history but also as a museum that the public can explore.

Visitors to North Point Lighthouse can climb the 74-foot tower to experience breathtaking panoramic views of Lake Michigan and the surrounding cityscape. Inside, the museum provides a dive into the rich history of the lighthouse and the life of its keepers through a variety of exhibits that include maritime artifacts, photographs, and historical documents. The lighthouse is an ideal destination for history buffs, maritime enthusiasts, or anyone looking for a picturesque spot to learn about Milwaukee's nautical heritage. Whether you're looking to delve into the fascinating past of lake navigation, enjoy a unique view of the lake, or simply want a picturesque setting for a leisurely afternoon, North Point Lighthouse offers an enriching and enjoyable experience for all ages. The lighthouse is open Saturday and Sunday year round from 1 pm to 4pm. There is an admission charge.

2650 North Wahl Avenue

northpointlighthouse.org

The Milwaukee Pierhead Lighthouse has been an active aid to navigation since its establishment in 1872, with the current structure operational since 1907. This iconic red lighthouse is situated at the end of the Milwaukee breakwater, marking the entrance to the Milwaukee River and Harbor. It's easily recognizable by its cylindrical steel structure painted in red, making it a popular subject for photographers. It is not open to the public, but you can walk to it.

East Erie Street (In Lakeshore State Park)

Milwaukee Breakwater Light stands proud over the Milwaukee Harbor. It is now on the National Register of Historic Places, is no longer operational, and owned by a private company. It is not open to the public and can only be viewed close up from the water.

Milwaukee Harbor

Visit Milwaukee's Favorite Beaches

Milwaukee's lakefront beaches are a delightful escape during the warmer months, providing a refreshing respite from city life. Here are two of the best beaches in Milwaukee, each offering unique features and activities:

Bradford Beach- Milwaukee's most popular beach. It's a hotspot for locals and visitors alike, featuring volleyball courts, a tiki bar, and ample space for sunbathing and swimming.

McKinley Beach- Offers a less crowded environment and beautiful views of the Milwaukee skyline. It's a great spot for swimming with a designated swimming area that is watched over by lifeguards during the summer months.

Milwaukee Art Museum

The Milwaukee Art Museum is a striking landmark, famous not only for its vast and varied collection but also for its breathtaking architectural design. The art museum is a must-see. Home to over 30,000 works of art, the museum spans four floors and features everything from ancient artifacts to contemporary pieces. Its dynamic architecture, designed by Santiago Calatrava, includes the movable "wings" of the Burke Brise Soleil that open and close daily. This museum is a hub of cultural enrichment and creativity, drawing art lovers and tourists alike to experience its exhibitions, educational programs, and special events. It's a cornerstone of Milwaukee's artistic community.

700 North Art Museum Drive

mam.org

Kayak On The River

For a fun and adventurous view of Milwaukee, go on a kayak tour or just rent one. Milwaukee Kayak Company offers various tours, from history tours to sunrise paddle tours. I have just rented a kayak and spent two hours enjoying the city from the water. There are also places along the river to stop, enjoy a beverage and lunch or dinner. For launch, rental, and tour information, see Milwaukee Kayak Company's website. (Photo page 74)

milwaukeekayak.com

Harley Davidson Museum

The Harley-Davidson Museum isn't just for motorcycle enthusiasts; it's a celebration of American innovation and culture. With its extensive collection of iconic motorcycles and memorabilia, the museum chronicles over a century of history that appeals to all, showcasing the evolution of design, engineering, and the spirit of the open road. You'll also find a bar and restaurant, a shop, and a Harley Davidson retail outlet inside the 20 acre campus.

400 West Canal Street

harley-davidson.com/museum

3rd Street Market Hall

Called 'Milwaukee's Kitchen Table', this food hall in the heart of downtown brings together an eclectic mix of local food vendors, offering a taste of Milwaukee's diverse culinary scene under one roof. From gourmet pizzas and Asian street food to artisan pastries and craft cocktails, there's something to satisfy every palate.

3rd Street Market Hall is also a community social space where family and friends can engage in a variety of activities like shuffleboard, ping pong, and mini-golf. Its open and modern design encourages interaction and exploration, with communal seating areas that invite guests to linger and enjoy the lively atmosphere.

275 West Wisconsin Avenue

3rdstmarkethall.com

Milwaukee Public Market

Featuring an array of local vendors, the Milwaukee Public Market offers everything from fresh seafood and gourmet cheeses to handcrafted confections and organic produce. It's not just a place to eat; it's a lively venue for experiencing cooking classes, seasonal events, and community gatherings. The market's open, airy space invites strolling and tasting, making it a perfect destination for food lovers and anyone looking to connect with the local culture. If you'd like a mini-tour of the downtown area you can ride **The Hop**, Milwaukee's free downtown streetcar that stops at key places along the route.

400 North Water Street

milwaukeepublicmarket.org

thehopmke.com

Stroll Around Historic Third Ward

After you walk around the public market, stroll around the historic 10 block stretch of shops, restaurants, and galleries that make up the Third Ward neighborhood. I will list a few of my favorite shops in the shopping section.

historicthirdward.org

The Milwaukee RiverWalk

The Milwaukee RiverWalk is a scenic urban pathway that winds along the Milwaukee River, offering a peaceful yet vibrant walking experience right in the heart of the city. Stretching over three miles, the RiverWalk seamlessly connects the Historic Third Ward, Downtown, and the Beerline B neighborhood (mostly residential), making it a prime route for exploring some of Milwaukee's most lively districts. Milwaukee's beloved **"Bronze Fonz"** takes up residence on the east side on the RiverWalk just south of Wells Street. It's a life-size statue of Henry Winkler's beloved character from 'Happy Days', the 1970's TV show set in Milwaukee. Seating areas, art installations, and a variety of shopping and restaurants dot the trail. (Photo page 74)

milwaukeeriverwalkdistrict.com

Best Place at the Historic Pabst Brewery

There are quite a few brewery tours you can do in Milwaukee. I will list some of them below, but I have a fond appreciation of Pabst, so if you are interested in learning about this iconic brand and its history, I urge you to take a history tour at Best Place at the Historic Pabst Brewery. During the tour, guests walk through the original Pabst corporate office and the historic Blue Ribbon Hall, adorned with intricate woodwork and stained glass, where they can learn about the evolution of Pabst and its impact on beer culture.

After the tour, visitors are encouraged to explore the vintage gift shop, which is stocked with a wide array of Pabst memorabilia—from classic beer cans and vintage advertisements to modern apparel and accessories. It's a perfect spot to pick up a souvenir that captures the essence of Pabst's rich heritage.

Adjacent to the gift shop is the inviting taproom, a cozy spot where guests can relax and sample a variety of Pabst beers. The taproom retains much of its original charm with elements that hark back to the brewery's early days. Here, visitors can enjoy a pint of classic Pabst Blue Ribbon or try some of the newer brews that are often exclusive to this location. The taproom also hosts a range of events, including live music nights, making it a vibrant part of Milwaukee's current beer scene. (Photo page 74)

917 West Juneau Avenue

nestplacemilwaukee.com

National Bobblehead Hall of Fame and Museum

The National Bobblehead Hall of Fame and Museum offers a whimsical and engaging experience that goes beyond typical museum visits. This one-of-a-kind institution is dedicated to the history and art of bobbleheads, featuring over 6,500 unique bobbleheads from various genres and eras, including sports, politics, entertainment, and more.

Visitors to the museum can explore the extensive collection, which includes some of the rarest and most unusual bobbleheads ever produced, as well as learn about the production process and the fascinating history behind these nodding figures. The museum also offers insights into how bobbleheads have become a popular collectible item and a part of pop culture. My favorites are the quirky TV celebrity and music bobbleheads. There is a huge selection of Wisconsin sport figures represented. Definitely a fun stop.

170 South 1st Street

bobbleheadhall.com

St. Joan Of Arc Chapel At Marquette University

For those who appreciate history intertwined with spiritual significance, the St. Joan of Arc Chapel at Marquette University is an essential visit. This medieval chapel, originally built in France in the 15th century, has a storied past involving St. Joan of Arc herself. Legend has it that she prayed before a certain stone, which now remains perpetually colder than its surroundings.

Transported stone by stone to the United States in the 1920s and eventually reconstructed on the Marquette campus in the 1960s, this chapel is not only a place of worship but also a remarkable piece of architectural history. Visitors can explore the intimate interior of the chapel and attend mass, or simply enjoy the peaceful ambiance of the surrounding gardens.

The chapel offers guided tours that delve into its rich history, architectural details, and the process of its transatlantic relocation. It is a peaceful retreat right in the heart of Milwaukee and offers a unique glimpse into medieval European history.

1421 West Wisconsin Avenue

marquette.edu/st-joan-of-arc-chapel

Attend A Festival

There's a reason why Milwaukee is also known as "The City of Festivals". Most of us have heard of Summerfest, the world's largest music festival held every summer along Milwaukee's lakefront. At $28 (2024) for a general admission ticket, you can get your fill of music from a wide range of genres from local acts to famous performers. You'll need to purchase a separate ticket for main stage acts. Summerfest is not the only festival held at the Henry Maier Festival Park. Here are some others:

Irish Fest

German Fest

Pride Fest

Festa Italiana

Polish Fest

Black Arts Fest

Mexican Fiesta

There are also a multitude of festivals held in other locations around the city. My favorite is Bastille Days held in Cathedral Square every July.

milwaukeeworldfestival.com

easttown.com/bastille-days

Black Cat Alley

Public art is all around Milwaukee, but this alley on the east side is an ode to what a neighborhood can do to transform a less than desirable space into an outdoor art gallery. There are 23 murals that adorn the walls in this private alley and other installations. It's become a popular spot for photographers.

Between Prospect Avenue and Ivanhoe behind the Oriental Theater. The entry at Ivanhoe is wheelchair accessible.

blackcatmke.com

Shopping

Boswell Book Company

Boswell Book Company is an independent bookstore beloved by locals for its wide range of titles and friendly, knowledgeable staff. The store hosts an impressive calendar of events, including author readings and book signings, making it a community hub for literary enthusiasts. I have attended author events here, and try to stop in whenever I am in Milwaukee. Whether you're looking for the latest bestseller or a rare find, Boswell's shelves are likely to hold a treasure waiting to be discovered.

2559 North Downer Avenue

boswellbooks.com

The Spice House

The Spice House is a culinary gem for those who love to cook and experiment with flavors. With an extensive array of spices, herbs, and seasonings sourced from around the world, it's a must-visit for both amateur cooks and professional chefs. Their expertly crafted blends can elevate any dish, making this store a key stop for enhancing your kitchen pantry. I love that they have Middle Eastern spices that can be hard to find elsewhere.

400 North Water Street (Public Market)

thespicehouse.com

Broadway Paper

For those passionate about fine paper and unique greeting cards, Broadway Paper is a paradise. The woman-owned store offers a wide selection of stationery, wedding invitations, and office supplies, all curated with a focus on design and quality. As someone who still prefers pen and paper to the keyboard, this store is a dream come true.

191 North Broadway

broadwaypaper.com

Edie Boutique

Edie Boutique is a chic boutique known for its trendy women's apparel and accessories. It offers a variety of fashionable items, from stylish handbags to seasonal attire, catering to those looking to keep up with the latest trends.

244 North Broadway

shopedie.com

Lela

Lela is a boutique in the Third Ward that blends clothing consignment with new boutique items, offering an eclectic mix of women's fashion. It's a great place for those who appreciate high style but also value sustainability and unique finds.

321 North Broadway

lelaboutique.com

Retique

Retique is a boutique thrift store operated by Goodwill, offering a curated selection of high-quality second-hand clothes and accessories. It's a fantastic place for fashion-conscious shoppers looking to find unique pieces without breaking the bank. Love this store.

190 North Broadway

amazinggoodwill.com/retique

Places To Eat and Drink In Milwaukee

Coffee and Bakery

Colectivo Coffee

Renowned for its quality and innovation, Colectivo Coffee is a staple in Milwaukee's coffee scene. With nine across the city, each café features uniquely vibrant atmospheres and architectural details. Colectivo roasts their own coffee, ensuring fresh and flavorful brews. Seasonal blends and locally sourced bakery items make this a favorite among locals. My favorite location is the one located right on the lakefront.

1701 North Lincoln Memorial Drive

colectivo.com

Amaranth Bakery & Cafe

Amaranth Bakery and Cafe excels in both savory and sweet offerings, with a focus on seasonal ingredients that ensure a fresh menu throughout the year. Known for their delicious scones, tarts, and quiches, this neighborhood gem provides a cozy setting, ideal for a morning coffee or a leisurely brunch.

3329 W Lisbon Avenue

Phone: (414) 934-0587

Blooming Lotus Gourmet Bakery

Blooming Lotus Bakery stands out in Milwaukee's bakery scene for its commitment to producing high-quality, wholesome baked goods that are both delicious and health-conscious. Using only natural sweeteners and no preservatives, the bakery offers a variety of breads, muffins, cookies, and cakes that cater to gluten-free and vegan diets without compromising on taste. Their cozy and inviting cafe space also serves excellent coffee, making it a perfect spot for a relaxing breakfast or a peaceful afternoon snack.

2215 East North Avenue

blbmke.com

Restaurants

Mader's Restaurant

Mader's Restaurant is one of Milwaukee's oldest and most famous German restaurants. It's been serving authentic German food since 1902, including schnitzel, sausages, and huge pretzels, Mader's also boasts an impressive collection of German art and armor. The restaurant's old-world charm and consistently excellent food have made it a favorite among generations of diners. I would suggest making a reservation, although I have enjoyed one of those massive pretzels at the bar. (Photo page 74)

1041 North Old World 3rd Street

madersrestaurant.com

AJ Bombers

AJ Bombers is a fun and energetic burger joint known for its peanut delivery system that drops peanuts right at your table. Their menu features creative burgers, loaded tater tots, and custard shakes, all at very reasonable prices. I've been told their cheese curds are some of the best in the city. It's a great spot for families or anyone looking for a casual and enjoyable meal.

1247 North Water Street

ajbombers.com

Bartolotta'sLake Park Bistro

Lake Park Bistro is in Milwaukee's scenic Lake Park and offers a fine dining experience with a French focus. Renowned for its authentic French dishes like Coq au Vin and Bouillabaisse, this restaurant provides a stunning view over Lake Michigan, making it perfect for a special occasion. I go when I want to feel like I am in Paris. Reservations suggested.

3133 East Newberry Boulevard

bartolottas.com/lake-park-bistro

La Merenda

La Merenda is a casual, internationally-inspired tapas bar that focuses on communal dining and small plates made from locally-sourced ingredients. The restaurant offers a vast array of dishes from around the world, allowing diners to sample many different flavors and styles in one visit. It's a great spot for groups looking to have a social dining experience.

125 East National Avenue

lamerenda125.com

Vanguard

Vanguard is known for its innovative approach to sausages, ranging from traditional bratwurst to more unique options like duck, bacon, and jalapeno. The bar-style setting and the option to customize your sausage with an array of toppings make Vanguard a fun and affordable dining choice.

2659 South Kinnickinnic Avenue

vanguardbar.com

Sobleman's

Sobelman's is famous throughout Milwaukee for its substantial burgers and Bloody Marys, each served with an over-the-top presentation. The restaurant prides itself on using fresh, quality ingredients, including locally sourced beef for their patties. Sobelman's offers a range of burgers, from classic cheeseburgers to unique creations loaded with various toppings like bacon, cheeses, and even stuffed jalapeños.

1900 West St Paul Avenue

soblemanspubandgrill.com

Bars, Wineries, and Breweries

There is no shortage of bars and breweries in Milwaukee. Beer lovers from around the world descend upon Milwaukee. After all, it is "Brew City". You can find a full list of bars and breweries on the Visit Milwaukee website. If you're interested in making brewery visits even more fun, you can also sign up for the Brew City Beer Pass on the website.

Milwaukee's downtown hotels also have bars and lounges open to the public. Listed are some of the best bar offerings for visitors around the city.

SafeHouse

SafeHouse is a spy-themed bar and restaurant that offers a truly unique and interactive experience. Hidden behind a nondescript doorway, patrons either need a password to enter or must perform a fun task. Inside, the espionage-themed decor and mystery provide a playful backdrop for enjoying innovative cocktails and pub fare. SafeHouse has been around since 1966 and is a must-visit for those looking for an experience that's out of the ordinary.

779 North Front Street

safe-house.com

Drink Wisconsinbly Pub

Drink Wisconsinbly has now made its home in the Deer District of Milwaukee just steps from Fiserv Forum, so it's positively packed on any Wisconsin sports game day. Drink Wisconsinbly Pub celebrates the state's culture and love for beer, cheese, and all things Wisconsin. This pub offers a jovial atmosphere where visitors can enjoy local beers and craft cocktails. It's a great spot to soak up Wisconsin's local pride and indulge in the state's fun drink-related souvenirs.

320 West Highland Avenue

wisconsinbly.com

Lakefront Brewery

A pioneer in the craft beer movement, Lakefront Brewery is known for its top ranked informative and entertaining brewery tours. Visitors can learn about the brewing process and the history of beer in Milwaukee, all while enjoying generous samples of Lakefront's diverse beer lineup. The brewery also features a riverside beer garden, making it a perfect spot on a sunny afternoon. You can also stop here during your kayak tour on the river.

1872 North Commerce Street

lakefrontbrewery.com

Urban Harvest Brewing Company

Urban Harvest has made a name for itself with its small-batch brews. Located in the Walker's Point neighborhood, it offers a cozy atmosphere where guests can enjoy craft beers. While the taproom serves snacks, they allow patrons to bring in food, or have it delivered from local Walker's Point restaurants.

1024 South 5th Street

urbanharvestbrewing.com

Sprecher Brewing Co.

Sprecher Brewing Co. is another cornerstone of Milwaukee's craft beer scene, known not only for its excellent beers but also for its gourmet sodas, including the famous Sprecher Root Beer. Visitors can tour the brewery to learn about the production processes of both their beers and sodas, making it an ideal visit for families or anyone interested in the craft of brewing. The gift shop offers a chance to take home some of these beloved beverages. It's a little north of the downtown area, but worth a stop at this iconic brewery.

701 West Glendale Avenue, Glendale

sprecherbrewery.com

The Tap Yard Beer Garden

Beer gardens are another fun, German-inspired beer experience. Milwaukee has quite a few. The Tap Yard has a beer garden along the river in Schlitz Park. How can you pass up a beer garden in a park named after a Milwaukee beer brand? There are events going on here nearly everyday in summer. Opened every May for the season.

1555 North Rivercenter Drive

thetapyards.com

Great Lakes Distillery

How about taking a break from beer for a bit? If you're looking for spirits, check out Great Lakes Distillery. Seriously... a drink called the Caramel Milwaukiatto? Mixed with the distillery's own bourbon whiskey? That's a wake up call, right? Great Lakes Distillery is a small-batch distillery that has garnered attention for its handcrafted spirits. Great Lakes Distillery produces a range of spirits including whiskey, gin, rum, and vodka, as well as unique offerings like absinthe and seasonal liqueurs. Visitors can take a tour, or enjoy a creative drinks menu serving both alcoholic and non-alcoholic cocktails.

616 West Virginia Street

greatlakesdistillery.com

Sweet Treats

Purple Door Ice Cream

I love ice cream, and gelato, and custard. It's that one common food item that I need to have at every destination I visit. Every single time I spend a day in Milwaukee, you are likely to find me at Purple Door at some point in my day. I adore its handcrafted ice creams in quirky flavors. How about beer and pretzels? Or what about balsamic vinegar? If you're more for traditional flavors, Purple Door has them too.

205 South 2nd Street

purpledooricecream.com

Kopp's Frozen Custard

Kopp's Frozen Custard is a beloved Milwaukee institution, renowned for its premium frozen custard and gigantic, flavor-packed burgers. Since its inception in 1950, Kopp's has been a cornerstone of the local dining scene, drawing both residents and visitors who come to indulge in its rich, creamy custard. Did you know that Kopp's was the first custard stand to start the "Flavor Of The Day"? Whether you go with the daily flavor or plain old vanilla, Kopp's Custard is a required stop on your way north out of Milwaukee.

5373 North Port Washington Road, Glendale

kopps.com

Accommodations

Hotels

Milwaukee, being an urban center, has thousands of hotels for your stay, including most chains. I just focus on favorite classic stays that are located right downtown.

The Pfister Hotel

The Pfister Hotel is a historic landmark and a symbol of Milwaukee's grandeur. Its history is captivating and each room has a copy of a book telling that story. Opened in 1893, it is famed for its opulent Victorian architecture and luxurious interiors. The hotel offers a range of accommodations from elegant rooms to lavish suites, all featuring modern amenities blended with old-world charm. The Pfister also houses a renowned spa, a rooftop lounge with panoramic views of the city, an artist in residence, and several dining options, making it a favorite for those seeking a refined experience.

424 East Wisconsin Avenue

thepfisterhotel.com

Saint Kate - The Arts Hotel

This is a unique boutique hotel that celebrates the arts in all its forms. Each room and space within the hotel is a canvas, showcasing work from local and national artists. The hotel features public gallery spaces, live performances, and workshops, making it a vibrant hub for creative guests and those who appreciate the arts. Saint Kate's central location also provides easy access to Milwaukee's theaters, museums, and downtown area. Even if you are not staying here, definitely go inside and walk around the public areas.

139 East Kilbourn Avenue

saintkatearts.com

Hilton Milwaukee City Center

An elegant high-rise hotel that combines historic charm with contemporary comfort. Its rooms offer all the modern amenities, while the architecture and decor reflect the 1920s Art Deco style. Located in the heart of downtown, the Hilton is conveniently connected to Milwaukee's convention center known as the Baird Center, formerly the Wisconsin Center. It's also close to many of Milwaukee's attractions, making it ideal for conference attendees and tourists alike.

509 West Wisconsin Avenue

hilton.com

Iron Horse Hotel

The Iron Horse Hotel is designed with a chic industrial aesthetic that nods to Milwaukee's manufacturing legacy. With an authentic gritty personality, it's especially popular among motorcycle enthusiasts, located near the Harley-Davidson Museum. The hotel caters to both business and leisure travelers with its spacious and stylish rooms, a library, a fitness center, and several dining options including a popular yard for social gatherings.

500 West Florida Street

theironhorsehotel.com

Port Washington

Just north of Milwaukee, Port Washington is a captivating harbor town brimming with history, charm, and scenic beauty. Its picturesque lakeside setting, combined with a rich maritime past, makes it a serene Wisconsin Harbor Town. One of my favorite things about Port Washington is its charming downtown area which gives off a distinct New England vibe. It offers fantastic shopping and dining. Whether you're a history enthusiast, a foodie, or just in search of a serene getaway, Port Washington promises an unforgettable experience.

Location

Port Washington is about 30 miles north from downtown Milwaukee and 30 miles south of Sheboygan along Lake Michigan. From Milwaukee take I-43 north.

Port Washington Facts

- Port Washington is often referred to as "The City of Seven Hills." This moniker draws comparisons to Rome, albeit on a smaller scale. The seven hills surround the city, and historically, they played a significant role in its development as neighborhoods and communities grew upon their terrains.

- Port Washington was initially known as Wisconsin's first "port of entry." Over the years, it has seen a flux of settlers, traders, and sailors, which contributed to its diverse cultural fabric.

- Founded by brothers Gilbert and Elmore Smith in the late 19th century, the Smith Bros. Fish Shanty was one of the most well-known commercial fishing enterprises on Lake Michigan. Apart from fishing, they expanded into diverse businesses, including a popular restaurant and coffee shop. The logo, depicting the two brothers, became an iconic representation of Port Washington's fishing heritage.

- Port Washington was the home of the Wisconsin Chair Company, founded in 1888. This company created the Paramount record label and was also responsible for inventing the wooden radio cabinet. The ingenuity and innovation of the city's residents played a pivotal role in shaping the town's industrial legacy.

- Today Port Washington's population is 12,614 (2021)

How Much Time To Spend In Port Washington

Depending on what you want to do, a day at the very minimum. If you want to take full advantage of the trails, shopping, and places to eat, a full weekend is suggested.

Things To Do In Port Washington

Port Washington Highlights

Port Washington Breaker Lighthouse

As an emblem of Port Washington's seafaring history, this art-deco lighthouse stands tall on the breakwater of the harbor. Tourists can stroll up to the lighthouse for an up-close view and photograph the stunning vistas of Lake Michigan. It is not open for tours, but its unique design offers a fabulous photo op.

311 E. Johnson Street

lighthousefriends.com/light.asp?ID=248

1860 Light Station

This meticulously restored light station gives visitors a glimpse into the life of a lighthouse keeper in the 19th century. Complete with period furnishings, this historical landmark serves as a museum offering guided tours. The Light Station is open seasonally and there is a small admission fee.

311 Johnson Street

pwhistory.org/1860-light-station

Upper Lake Park

Overlooking Lake Michigan, this park is a serene spot with picnic areas, playgrounds, and a spectacular view of the Port Washington Lighthouse. This park is home to many of Port Washington's events throughout the year. It's a favorite for both locals and visitors for relaxation and recreational activities. Don't forget to take the 83 steps down to the Lake Michigan shoreline.

554 N. Lake Street

portwashington.recdesk.com

Coal Dock Park

A newer addition to Port Washington's parks, the Coal Dock Park offers a wonderful walking trail right by the lake, bird-watching platforms, and interpretive signage about the area's ecology and history. There is also a promenade and bridge that will take you to the Port Washington Avian Sanctuary and Port Washington South Beach Park.

146 S Wisconsin Street

portwashington.recdesk.com

Ozaukee Interurban Trail

This 30-mile trail, running through Port Washington, provides a scenic route following the path of a historic railway. It's perfect for walking, running, or biking, offering picturesque views and connecting various towns and natural spots. It is open for full-year usage, making it great for cross-country skiing in the winter.

interurbantrail.com

Shopping

Bernie's Fine Meats

Established in 1941, Bernie's is a legendary establishment offering a variety of gourmet meats, sausages, and local specialties. Their award-winning beef jerky is a must-try, and their selection of local cheeses, seasonings, and delicacies make it a food lover's paradise. The perfect stop to grab supplies for a picnic in one park in Port Washington.

119 N. Franklin Street

berniesfinemeats.com

Eclectic Avenue

You'll find work from local artisans, crystals, oracle cards, natural body products, and a whole lot more at Eclectic Avenue.

226 North Franklin Street

eclectic-avenue-llc.business.site

Locally Inspired

Make gift-giving simple by stopping in this shop. Curated items from Wisconsin makers fill Locally Inspired. They pride themselves in not only supporting local artisans, but creating a space of community.

226 E. Main Street

locallyinspiredwi.com

Duluth Trading

It may not be a one-of-a-kind shop, but Duluth Trading is a big draw for shoppers downtown. The store makes its Port Washington home inside the historical Smith Bros. Fish Shanty Restaurant. Duluth Trading is known for its rugged work clothing and gear. You'll find a huge selection and friendly staff here.

108 N. Franklin Street

duluthtrading.com

Places To Eat And Drink In Port Washington

Coffee and Bakery

Daily Baking Company

Renowned for its fresh, daily-made artisanal breads and pastries, the Daily Baking Company is a cornerstone of Port Washington's café culture. Step into this warm and inviting space to enjoy a perfect espresso, a flaky croissant, or one of their specialty sourdough loaves. Their commitment to quality ingredients and traditional baking techniques shines through in every bite. This one is definitely one of our favorites.

211 N. Franklin Street

dailybakingcompany.com

Java Dock Café

It's the ideal spot to enjoy a rich latte or a robust cup of joe sourced from the finest local coffee roasters like Collectivo and Valentine. They also offer a selection of homemade sandwiches, soups, and bakery items that are perfect for breakfast or lunch. The casual and friendly atmosphere makes it a favorite among locals and visitors alike.

116 W Grand Avenue

.javadockcafe.com

Dockside Deli

Dockside Deli may be known for its sandwiches, but their coffee and baked goods shouldn't be overlooked. Offering stunning views of the marina, this deli has a selection of pastries and desserts that are made in-house, complemented by a full coffee bar serving classic and seasonal beverages. Whether it's for a quick snack or a leisurely break, Dockside Deli welcomes you with its friendly service and comfortable seating.

218 E Main Street

docksidedeli.com

Restaurants

Twisted Willow Restaurant

Twisted Willow is a family-owned restaurant that provides a farm-to-table dining experience. This establishment takes pride in sourcing its ingredients from local farms and suppliers, ensuring that each dish served is of the highest quality and freshness. The restaurant offers a seasonal menu that includes savory steaks, fresh seafood, and vegetarian options, all crafted with a twist of innovation. The ambiance combines rustic charm with a touch of elegance, making it suitable for a casual dinner or a special occasion.

308 N Franklin Street

twistedwillowrestaurant.com

The Pasta Shoppe

For those who cherish Italian cuisine, The Pasta Shoppe is a must-visit. This cozy eatery is known for its hearty portions, homemade pasta, and traditional Italian dishes. From classic spaghetti and meatballs to more adventurous seafood pasta dishes, there's something to please every palate. An excellent selection of wines that pair perfectly with their flavorful dishes complements their warm and welcoming atmosphere.

323 N Franklin Street

portpastashoppe.com

Moonlight Tavern

Inside the Port Hotel, Moonlight Tavern offers a fine dining experience in an elegant and historic setting. Known for its prime rib and steak selections, the restaurant also provides an impressive list of wines. The Moonlight Tavern is ideal for a romantic dinner or celebrating a special occasion, providing a sophisticated atmosphere and attentive service that will make your evening memorable.

101 E Main Street

moonlighttavernattheporthotel.com

Bars, Wineries, and Breweries

Vines To Cellar

Vines to Cellar is a small boutique winery located in the heart of downtown Port Washington. Visitors can expect a warm, welcoming atmosphere perfect for both novice and experienced wine enthusiasts. The winery offers a diverse selection of wines, with tastings available to help you find your perfect bottle. They also provide custom labeling services, which can make for a unique gift or a memorable souvenir. For those interested in the winemaking process, Vines to Cellar offers a "make your own wine" experience complete with bottling and labeling. How cool!

114 E Main St

vinestocellar.com

Inventors Brewpub

Located on the lakefront with an excellent view of Lake Michigan, Inventors Brewpub is a destination for those who enjoy craft beer with a side of innovation. The brewery has a friendly, inventive atmosphere where each beer tells a story of local history or a nod to the inventive spirit. Their lineup includes a range of styles, from refreshing lagers to robust stouts, and they often feature live music and community events. The brewpub also serves up a menu of classic pub fare with a local twist.

435 N Lake Street

inventorsbrewpub.com

Sweet Treats

The Chocolate Chisel

Calling all chocolate lovers! The Chocolate Chisel is your paradise.. This artisanal chocolate shop crafts its treats in small batches, using fine ingredients. Visitors can watch chocolate being made and choose from a variety of confections such as truffles, chocolate bars, and specialty items. The shop's old-world charm and the intoxicating smell of chocolate ensure a delightful sensory experience. As if all that chocolate isn't enough, you can get small batch handmade ice cream here by Amazing Ice Cream Co. (Photo page 74)

125 W Grand Avenue

chocolatechisel.com

Accommodations

Hotels

Port Hotel Residence Inn

The Port Hotel Residence Inn is a boutique hotel that offers a blend of historic charm and modern amenities. It is well-known for its elegant rooms, some of which offer views of Lake Michigan. Guests can expect a high level of service, luxury bedding, and a complimentary gourmet breakfast. The hotel's restaurant is a fine dining destination in its own right.

101 E. Main Street

theporthotel.com

The Harborview

As its name suggests, The Harborview offers stunning views of the harbor and Lake Michigan. Guests can enjoy a range of amenities, including an indoor pool, on-site restaurant, and a fitness center. The hotel has a variety of room types to meet different needs and budgets.

135 E. Grand Avenue

choicehotels.com

Campgrounds

Harrington Beach State Park

Just a short drive north of Port Washington, Harrington Beach State Park offers a more natural and rustic stay admiring the beauty of Wisconsin's landscape. The campground provides both basic and electric hookup sites suitable for tents and RVs. Amenities include picnic areas, clean shower facilities, and easy access to the park's mile-long beach on Lake Michigan. Guests can enjoy hiking, bird watching, and stargazing at the observatory. A note about Wisconsin State Parks:

A sticker is required for entry into Harrington State Park. Also, campsites at all state parks fill up fast, so be sure and book early.

531 County Road D, Belgium

dnr.wisconsin.gov/topic/parks/harringtonbeach

Sheboygan

Sheboygan is my home base. I live just 20 miles west of the city, so I know it well. I have especially enjoyed seeing Sheboygan grow into a premier destination in Wisconsin. When people ask me where they should visit in Wisconsin besides the likely tourist spots of Door County, Wisconsin Dells, and Milwaukee, I recommend Sheboygan.

We know Sheboygan as the "Malibu of the Midwest". Because of its unique shoreline jutting out into Lake Michigan, surfers around the world covet the waves in winter. Head to Deland Park anytime there is a windy day from August to April (peak surfing season, although you can surf year-round) and chances are, you will see surfers braving the chilly, often frigid winter temperatures riding the waves.

Sheboygan is also known as the "Bratwurst Capital Of The World". You can come celebrate that famous sausage anytime, but the best time is during Brat Days, an annual summer event put on by the Sheboygan Jaycees. I'll also share where you can get the best traditional brat in Sheboygan.

Sheboygan has transformed from the city I knew growing up. Today's Sheboygan is a destination filled with arts, a walkable downtown area, lots of shopping, a foodies paradise, and exceptional beach areas. You will find plenty to do here.

Location

Sheboygan is an easy drive right up I-43, about a half hour north of Port Washington.

Sheboygan Facts

- Sheboygan was officially incorporated in 1846. German, Dutch, and Irish immigrants who settled in the area contributed to its diverse cultural heritage, and significantly influenced the city's growth.

- Sheboygan's location along Lake Michigan made it a significant port in the 19th century. The city was a key player in the shipping and shipbuilding industries, which were vital to the region's economy.

- In the late 19th and early 20th centuries, Sheboygan became known as "Chair City" because of its prominence in the furniture industry. Companies like the Phoenix Chair Company and Crocker Chair Company were major employers in the city.

- Sheboygan is home to several historic landmarks, including Indian Mound Park, which preserves ancient Native American burial mounds, and the Sheboygan County Historical Museum, which showcases the city's rich history.

- As of 2021, Sheboygan's population stands at approximately 48,180.

How Much Time To Spend In Sheboygan

I know I'm a little biased, but you could easily spend a whole week taking in most of the sights in Sheboygan and the surrounding area. The cute nearby villages of Kohler (yes THAT Kohler) and Elkhart Lake are each worthy of a day to explore.

Since this book is specifically covering Wisconsin Harbor Towns, I will leave those places out of this guide, especially since there is so much to do in Sheboygan on its own.

Things To Do In Sheboygan

Sheboygan offers visitors a wide range of things to do. From sailing lessons to the world-renowned John Michael Kohler Arts Center, your getaway to Sheboygan will be filled with interesting adventures. I highly suggest stopping in at the Visit Sheboygan Visitors Center. You can get lots of information from the staff, and pick up print information as well. Check out the huge inventory of Sheboygan-themed clothing and cool things from local artisans.

Visit Sheboygan Visitors Center

826 South 8th Street

visitsheboygan.com

Sheboygan Highlights

Lighthouses

Sheboygan Breakwater Lighthouse- A visit to Deland Park and the harbor area will lead you to the cement breakwall where you can walk all the way to the lighthouse. Although not typically open for public tours, its presence adds a unique charm to the Sheboygan shoreline, making it a must-see for visitors. The red lighthouse, with its classic design, offers a glimpse into the maritime history of Sheboygan and serves as a symbol of the town's long standing relationship with the Great Lakes. Whether viewed from the land or the water, the Sheboygan Lighthouse is an enduring emblem of Wisconsin's nautical heritage.

Broughton Drive

lighthousefriends.com/light.asp?ID=249

Bookworm Gardens

Bookworm Gardens is a botanical garden based on popular children's books, and although your kids will love it, it is 100 percent enjoyable for adults too. It is my favorite place in Sheboygan (besides the beaches). Bookworm Gardens is an oasis, a place to come to admire the flowers and plants, as well as a place of reflection. It's a reminder that we can all view the world with childlike splendor and leave the stress of everyday life behind, even for an afternoon. Each individual garden is modeled after a classic children's book. Each section of the garden has copies of those books for you to take and read. There are interactive exhibits, a vegetable garden, and The Three Bears. Bookworm Gardens also hosts annual events. This is a must-stop on your visit.

1415 Campus Drive

bookwormgardens.org

John Michael Kohler Art Preserve

This unique destination is more than just an art museum; it's an immersive experience that intertwines nature, art, and the profound legacy of visionary artists. The Art Preserve focuses on "art environments" – comprehensive artistic expressions that encompass an artist's surroundings and way of life. It's a celebration of folk artists, those among us who turn their living spaces into masterpieces. Featuring over 37,000 square feet of gallery space, each permanent artist has a dedicated space, created to give the visitor a sampling of the true environment of the artist. What I find fascinating is the glimpse into the minds of these artists. Most were untrained and worked with materials easily and cheaply available, like glass, stone, and even chicken bones.

Entry to the museum is free and you can make a reservation to visit although it is not required. Don't miss the bathrooms. (Photo page 123)

3636 Lower Falls Road

jmkac.org/art-preserve

James Tellen Woodland Sculpture Garden

A walk through this peaceful wooded property immerses the visitor into a real-life artist environment. Visit this serene garden before or after you go to the John Michael Kohler Art Preserve to really appreciate this place. You'll find more than 30 different sculptures, many with a religious theme sprinkled on the property. The characters are almost lifelike, adding to the mystic feel of the property. It's a place to reflect and feel the natural environment around you. Today the cottage serves as a temporary accommodation for artists in residence. No admission and open from dawn to dusk.

5634 Evergreen Drive

kohlerfoundation.org/preservation/preserved-sites/tellen-woodland-sculpture-garden

Take A Surfing Lesson

Since you're in the "Malibu of the Midwest" why not pick up a new skill? I suggest taking a 2-hour surf class available through **EOS Surf Shop**. You may have to have a few adventurous bones in your body, but it's a great checkmark on your bucket list. EOS also rents surfboards, paddle boards, kayaks, and all the gear needed. If you'd rather not try surfing yourself, you can always watch the surfers from shore when the conditions are right, usually the winter months.

510 North 8th Street

eossurf.com

Acuity Flagpole

Anyone driving near Sheboygan on I-43, can't help but notice the enormous American flag, proudly welcoming visitors to the area. That is the Acuity Flagpole. The flagpole is 400 feet tall, flying an American flag that is 70 by 140 feet. It's the world's tallest symbol of freedom (as of this writing). You can actually get up close to it at any time. The flag weighs 250 pounds and does not fly during severe weather or high winds. Surrounding the base of the flagpole are pavers commemorating Sheboygan County residents killed in active duty from the Civil War to present day.

2800 Taylor Drive

acuity.com/about/flagpole

Kohler Andrae State Park

Kohler Andrae State Park is one of the most popular state parks in Sheboygan. It has one of the best Lake Michigan beaches, the two mile Dune Cordwalk, a campground, picnic shelters, the Sanderling Nature Center, and did I mention the beach? There are a total of seven trails in the park and plenty of outdoor activities to enjoy. The marsh is great for birdwatchers, and bikers will find a 2 ½ mile trail, along with plenty of roads to navigate. You'll also find picnic areas, a fishing pier, and the nature center. Many areas are wheelchair-friendly, and the park even has two beach wheelchairs available. You just need to call the park.

Admission requires a Wisconsin State Park Sticker, or day pass. (Photo page 123)

1020 Beach Park Lane

dnr.wisconsin.gov/topic/parks/kohlerandrae

John Michael Kohler Arts Center

The arts are alive in Sheboygan, which is definitely evident when you are downtown. Murals are everywhere, the beautiful City Green hosts events, and one of the real gems is the John Michael Kohler Arts Center. The Arts Center hosts an ever-changing list of exhibitions in all mediums, and ongoing events, so it's usually a flurry of activity. Visitors will also find a cafe, a shop, and you MUST visit the restrooms to see why they've been chosen as the world's best.

608 New York Avenue

jmkac.org

Farmers Market

Wednesday and Saturday mornings are busy in Fountain Park in the downtown area. The weekly farmers market not only has fruit and vegetable stands, but farm-raised meat, cheese, honey, and fresh flowers. You'll also find food vendors and artists selling their wares. The markets open in June and run through fall.

8th and Erie Streets Fountain Park

sheboygancountyinterfaith.org/farmers-market

Deland Park

This lakeside park is one of the favorite parks of locals and visitors in Sheboygan. Its location on Lake Michigan makes it a favorite for swimmers, surfers, and those who want to enjoy the sparkling blue waters. There is a play area for the kids and volleyball nets set up on the beach in summer. This park is also home to many events throughout the year like the 4th of July celebration and more. This is also the final resting spot of the remains of the **Lottie Cooper,** a three-masted schooner that sank in 1894. The shipwreck was rediscovered before construction of the current marina in 1992. (Photo page 123)

901 Broughton Drive

> **Wisconsin Shipwreck Coast National Marine Sanctuary**
>
> In 2021, a vast 962 miles of Lake Michigan coastline from Port Washington north to just above the Kewaunee County line was designated as the Wisconsin Shipwreck Coast National Marine Sanctuary. This includes the harbor towns of Port Washington, Sheboygan, Manitowoc, and Two Rivers. There are 36 known shipwrecks and a suspected 60 more within the boundaries of the underwater sanctuary. Twenty-seven of those 36 shipwrecks are listed on the National Register of Historical Places. Since Sheboygan is in the middle of communities that are home to the sanctuary, it's listed in this chapter. There are ongoing talks and plans between sanctuary communities about what role the sanctuary can play in terms of tourism for these Wisconsin Harbor Towns.
> sanctuaries.noaa.gov/wisconsin

Stephanie H Weill Center For The Performing Arts

This beautifully restored 1928 historic theater, originally a vaudeville house and movie palace, now serves as a vibrant venue for a wide array of performances, ranging from live music and theater to dance and film. The Weill Center is not just a place to witness great art; it's a cornerstone of Sheboygan's cultural identity. Throughout the year, the center brings in national acts, and amazing plays, as well as local community events.

826 North 8th Street

weillcenter.com

Ellwood H May Environmental Park (Maywood)

This park is an outdoor sanctuary with six different habitats, trails, and an Ecology Center. There are 135 acres to explore. Grab a map of the park and follow the trails to look for all the bird species listed. How many can you find? The park hosts many events and programs for all ages. There is no entry fee.

3615 Mueller Road

gomaywood.org

Shopping

WordHaven BookHouse

Probably my favorite bookstore anywhere. Owner CJ has created an inclusive and welcoming refuge for all book lovers. WordHaven BookHouse offers a wide selection of genres, from bestsellers to rare finds. It's a perfect spot for those seeking a quiet escape into the world of literature. The store also hosts weekly events, reading, and workshops.

923 North 8th Street

wordhaven-bookhouse.com/wordhaven

Olivu 426

Specializing in natural skincare and wellness products, Olivu 426 offers a range of handmade items from essential oils to custom skincare solutions, all crafted with care and quality ingredients.

502 North 8th Street

olivu426.com

Stefano's Slo Food Market

A local favorite for fresh, organic, and locally-sourced food products. Slo Food Market is a great place to find artisanal cheeses, organic produce, and other gourmet items. Not only is it a market, but you can grab a ready-made meal from the hot case, or a yummy cookie from the bakery. There's some seating inside to enjoy a cup of coffee and your lunch.

731 Pennsylvania Avenue

slofoodmarket.com

Nikki's Nex To New

An upscale consignment shop, Nikki's Nex To New offers a variety of new and gently used clothing, and accessories for everyone. It's a treasure trove for sustainable shopping.

1019 North 8th Street

nikkisnex2new.com

Victorian Chocolate Shoppe

Indulge in the rich, sweet flavors of handcrafted chocolates at the Victorian Chocolate Shoppe. This charming store offers a delightful assortment of chocolates, truffles, and confectioneries. You'll also find a huge selection of old-time candy.

519 South 8th Street

victorianchocolateshoppe.com

The GameBoard

An ideal spot for board game enthusiasts, The GameBoard features a vast collection of puzzles and games, from classics to the latest releases. It also has a selection of toys, candles and other interesting merchandise.

621 North 8th Street

the-gameboard.myshopify.com

Relish

A culinary delight, Relish offers an array of kitchen gadgets, cookware, and unique cooking classes. Perfect for those who love to cook or are looking for a unique gift.

811 North 8th Street

relishkitchenstore.com

Places To Eat And Drink In Sheboygan

Sheboygan is a food lover's paradise. From the upscale Italian restaurants like Lino Ristorante and Trattoria Stephano, to local favorites Sly's Midtown Saloon and Harry's Diner, the eating options are endless.

Coffee and Bakery

Paradigm Coffee & Music

Paradigm Coffee and Music is not just a coffee shop; it's a cultural hub in Sheboygan. Known for its eclectic and inviting atmosphere, it serves high-quality coffee and a variety of delicious eats. Paradigm also doubles as a venue for local music and art, making it a favorite spot for those who appreciate creativity alongside their caffeine.

1202 North 8th Street

paradigmvenue.com

Weather Center Cafe

This charming cafe not only serves excellent coffee but also offers a great selection of breakfast and lunch options. The Weather Center Cafe is known for its friendly staff and the warm, welcoming environment it provides for customers. Its location along the river makes for a relaxing view from the outside tables in summer.

809 Riverfront Drive

Phone: (920) 459-9283

City Bakery

City Bakery stands out for its Sheboygan hard rolls, delectable artisan bread, pastries, and cakes. The bakery prides itself on using the finest ingredients and traditional baking methods, ensuring a taste that is both authentic and satisfying. It's arguably the best classic bakery in Sheboygan.

1102 Michigan Avenue

sheboygancitybakery.com

Johnston's Bakery

Johnston's Bakery is a delightful spot known for its delicious, freshly-baked goods. From scrumptious donuts to mouth-watering pastries, this bakery offers a wide variety of treats that are sure to satisfy any sweet tooth. Their commitment to quality and tradition since 1950 makes every visit a delightful experience. The old-time atmosphere is worth a visit.

1227 Superior Avenue

johnstonsbakery.com

Sunday Dough

Sunday Dough brings a new level of sweetness to Sheboygan with its delightful array of donuts. From classic favorites to innovative flavors, each donut is a work of art. It's a must-visit for those who love to start their day with a touch of sugar and joy.

1402 South 8th Street

sundaydough.com

West Side Bakery

By now it may be obvious to you that hometown bakeries rule Sheboygan. Each local has a favorite for its hard rolls and other baked goods. West Side Bakery is known for its warm, homely feel and scrumptious baked goods. Whether you're in the mood for a flaky pastry or a decadent cake, West Side Bakery has it all, made with love and quality ingredients.

1422 Indiana Avenue

Phone: (920) 457-3313

Restaurants

Lino Ristorante Italiano

Named after its charming Italian owner, Lino Ristorante Italiano is known for its authentic Italian dishes, crafted with passion and finesse. The restaurant's ambiance transports you to Italy with its warm, inviting décor. Enjoy a selection of pasta, seafood, and other Italian specialties, all paired perfectly with their extensive wine list. Reservations are recommended.

422 South Pier Drive

linoitalia.com

Trattoria Stefano

Trattoria Stefano is a delightful high-end Italian restaurant that brings authentic flavors to Sheboygan. Known for its fresh ingredients and homemade pasta, the restaurant offers a cozy, intimate atmosphere perfect for a romantic dinner or a family gathering. Expect classic Italian dishes with a modern twist. Reservations are recommended.

522 North 8th Street

trattoriastefano.com

Black Pig

The Black Pig takes comfort food to a new level. This restaurant offers a menu filled with flavorful, creative dishes, all made from locally-sourced ingredients. The relaxed yet elegant setting makes it ideal for a casual lunch or a sophisticated dinner. The White Truffle Fries are the best fries around.

821 North 8th Street

eatblackpig.com

Sly's Midtown Salooon

Sly's Midtown Salooon offers a casual dining experience in the heart of Sheboygan. Known for its lively dive bar atmosphere, it's a great spot for enjoying classic

American pub fare, from juicy burgers to delicious wings, in a friendly setting. Remember how I had a place in mind for a traditional brat? Sly's is where you can find the classic Brat Plate. It's a must! You'll thank me for an authentic Sheboygan culinary experience. Also, you cannot beat the prices. (photo page 123)

508 North 8th Street

slysbarandgrill.com

Majerle's Black River Grill

Majerle's Black River Grill is a favorite for those seeking a cozy supper club dining atmosphere with a menu full of comforting classics. This grill is particularly known for its hearty dishes, welcoming service, and warm ambiance and wildlife viewing out the big window.

5033 Evergreen Drive

blackrivergrill.com

Parker John's

Parker John's is renowned for its mouth-watering barbecue and pizza, making it a must-visit for fans of American comfort food. With a focus on quality ingredients and authentic flavors, it's a great place for a casual meal with family and friends. Fabulous riverfront seating and live music on the deck in summer. A definite favorite among locals and visitors.

705 Riverfront Drive

parkerjohns.com/sheboygan

Seebooth Delicatessen

Seeboth Delicatessen offers a delightful selection of breakfasts, sandwiches, salads, and more. This delicatessen is perfect for a quick, tasty lunch, especially if you're looking for quality deli fare. They also have fresh baked goods and huge cookies at the counter. I recommend the Tat-Chos for a hearty breakfast.

1501 South 8th Street

seebothdeli.com

Il Ritrovo

Il Ritrovo is a certified Neapolitan pizzeria, offering a fantastic array of wood-fired pizzas. This eatery not only serves up delicious pizzas but also offers a variety of Italian antipasti, salads, and desserts. The lively ambiance and authentic Italian flavors are not to be missed. A must for pizza lovers.

515 South 8th Street

ilritrovopizza.com

Field To Fork

Field to Fork, as the name suggests, focuses on farm-to-table dining. This café provides a unique experience where you can enjoy freshly prepared meals made with organic and sustainable ingredients. The atmosphere is lively. I usually end up with either the quiche or avocado toast with poached egg.

511 South 8th Street

fieldtoforkcafe.com

Harry's Diner

Harry's Diner takes you back in time with its classic diner setting. Known for serving up traditional American breakfast and lunch dishes, this diner is ideal for those looking for a nostalgic and hearty meal. It's a local hot spot.

2504 Calumet Drive

Phone: (920) 458-5200

Bars, Wineries, And Breweries

3 Sheeps Brewing Company

3 Sheeps Brewing Company is a must-visit for craft beer enthusiasts. Known for their creative and diverse beer selections, this brewery offers a welcoming tasting room where visitors can sample their unique brews. The atmosphere is casual and pet friendly, perfect for a relaxed evening out.

1837 North Avenue

3sheepsbrewing.com

8th Street Ale House

8th Street Ale Haus is a favorite local spot for craft beer lovers. Offering a wide range of beers on tap, including many local and regional brews, it's a place where you can explore new flavors in a cozy, pub-like atmosphere. They also serve hearty pub fare, along with live music and open mic nights, making it a great spot for a casual night out.

1132 North 8th Street

8thstreetalehaus.com

Urbane

Urbane could easily have been listed under restaurants, but if you're in the mood for craft cocktails, it rules the day. Urbane is a stylish bar offering a sophisticated ambiance. Known for its craft cocktails and chic decor, it's the perfect place for an evening of upscale relaxation. The skilled bartenders at Urbane can craft a drink to suit any taste, making it a favorite among locals and visitors.

1231 North 8th Street

urbanesheboygan.com

Sweet Treats

Blast Soft Serve

Blast Soft Serve is known for its delicious and creamy soft-serve ice cream. Offering a variety of flavors and toppings, it's a fantastic spot for families and anyone looking to enjoy a classic ice cream treat. Window service only. The fun, laid-back atmosphere makes it a local favorite during the warmer months. Oh and it's my favorite local spot for Dole Whip. Open seasonally only.

406 Pennsylvania Avenue

Phone: (920) 453-0011

South Pier Parlor

South Pier Parlor is the place to satisfy your ice cream craving. Known for its wide variety of flavors and generous servings, it's a perfect place to enjoy a classic ice cream cone while strolling along the riverfront. The friendly, old-fashioned atmosphere makes every visit enjoyable.

434 South Pier Drive

southpierparlor.com

Accommodations

There are a number of chain hotels located in and around Sheboygan. Here are my recommendations.

Hotels

Blue Harbor Resort

Blue Harbor is a destination unto itself. To have a room facing Lake Michigan and an amazing sunrise view is magical. Blue Harbor Resort is a lakeside retreat known for its spacious rooms and suites. The resort also features an indoor waterpark, making it a perfect destination for families. Guests can enjoy a range of amenities including a spa, dining options, and easy access to the lakefront and the incredible beaches.

725 Blue Harbor Drive

blueharborresort.com

Harbor Winds Hotel

Harbor Winds Hotel provides a serene and comfortable stay, with a riverfront location that allows easy access to the downtown area. The hotel is known for its friendly service and clean, comfortable rooms.

905 South 8th Street

stayharborwinds.com

Watershed Hotel

This new boutique hotel property is on the river and has 25 rooms available. The hotel has an industrial modern feel. All the rooms have a refrigerator and microwave, and there is event space indoors and outside. The downtown location is great for walking to restaurants and shopping.

838 North 15th Street

watershedsheboygan.com

Campgrounds

Kohler Andrae State Park

There are 137 sites, 52 are electric, and one accessible cabin in Kohler Andrae State Park. Many of the sites are wooded. There are also two group camping areas inside the park. This campground is very popular and books out 11 months in advance. This is one of my favorite Wisconsin state campgrounds. The campground has two shower houses with flush toilets and numerous vault toilets. There is a dump station.

1020 Beach Park Lane

dnr.wisconsin.gov/topic/parks/kohlerandrae/recreation/camping

Manitowoc

Manitowoc is more than just a city—it's a living museum of maritime heritage surrounded by lush farmland. While Manitowoc is very much an industrial city, it has many gems that entice visitors to explore.

I made the half-hour drive nearly every day from my home to Manitowoc during the 32 years I spent working at a local manufacturing company. It became a tourist destination during that time with the addition of the SS Badger Car Ferry that connects Manitowoc and Ludington, Michigan, Manitowoc. That prompted the opening of many unique restaurants and businesses, joining longtime established businesses. The ferry, the Manitowoc Maritime Museum, and the Capitol Civic Center have revitalized the downtown area, primarily on and around 8th street.

Besides the lure of the downtown area, there is ample opportunity for outdoor recreation in Manitowoc. The Ice Age National Scenic Trail runs through a portion of the city, and the well-used Maritime Trail runs along the lakeshore connecting Manitowoc and Two Rivers. Like many of our harbor towns, Manitowoc also has a thriving charter fishing community.

The official tourism entity in Manitowoc is the **Manitowoc Area Visitors and Convention Bureau**.

manitowoc.info

Location

Manitowoc is about a half hour north of Sheboygan. Accessing Manitowoc is easy via I-43, or you can take a more scenic route by getting on Lakeshore Drive from Sheboygan as it follows along the lakeshore.

Manitowoc Facts

- During World War II, Manitowoc played a significant role in the war effort by building 28 submarines. These subs were known as "Freshwater Submarines" because Manitowoc was the only freshwater port to build submarines. Today, the legacy continues with annual events celebrating this maritime history, including submarine veterans' reunions.

- Once the largest manufacturer of aluminum cookware in the world, the Mirro Aluminum Company was founded in Manitowoc in 1909. It played a crucial role in shaping the local economy and even contributed to the war efforts by manufacturing aluminum parts for military use.

- After Tom Gannon, the toy sales manager for Manitowoc's Aluminum Specialty Company, observed a metal Christmas tree on display in downtown Chicago, he was inspired to bring the concept back to Manitowoc. The original tree, crafted in Chicago by Metal Coatings Inc., was both heavy and costly. Recognizing an opportunity, a company engineer designed an innovative, lightweight version using aluminum, making it more affordable. In 1959, the company debuted their Evergleam Christmas tree at the American Toy Fair. The Evergleam quickly became the most popular aluminum tree of its era and remains a coveted collectible to this day.

- In a quirky twist of history, a piece of the Soviet satellite Sputnik IV crashed in Manitowoc in 1962, marking the town in space history. The city celebrates by holding an annual event to mark the date.

- William Rahr, a German immigrant, began the Eagle Brewery in Manitowoc after settling here in 1847. He began making malt barley soon after and selling it to area breweries. The company sold malt barley to Anheuser-Busch beginning in 1891, eventually selling the Manitowoc facility to Anheuser-Busch in 1962. The grain storage towers visible at the end of Washington Street became a part of Manitowoc's city landscape.

- Today the population of Manitowoc is 34,570 (2022)

How Much Time To Spend In Manitowoc

You can see most of Manitowoc's highlights during a long weekend. If you want to spend more of a relaxing visit here, you can easily stay a week and then take in the surrounding area and the recreational opportunities the city offers.

Things To Do In Manitowoc

Manitowoc Highlights

Lighthouse

Manitowoc Breakwater Light- This iconic lighthouse, not open to the public but accessible by a walk along the breakwater, offers stunning views of Lake Michigan and the Manitowoc skyline. A must-visit for photography enthusiasts and history buffs alike. Please take caution and do not walk out to the lighthouse in bad weather.

425 Maritime Drive

lighthousefriends.com/light.asp?ID=250

Wisconsin Maritime Museum

Explore a pivotal piece of maritime history at the Wisconsin Maritime Museum, the largest museum dedicated to the Great Lakes. Visitors can immerse themselves in the heroic tales of WWII submarines, notably through a detailed tour of the USS Cobia, a fully restored submarine moored in the harbor. The museum's extensive exhibits span model ships, maritime artifacts, and interactive displays that appeal to all ages, making it a profound educational and engaging experience. The museum has just opened up a new exhibit spotlighting the Wisconsin Shipwreck Coast National Marine Sanctuary (read more in the Sheboygan chapter) from the historical perspective.

75 Maritime Drive

wisconsinmaritime.org

Rahr-West Art Museum

Delight in artistic brilliance at the Rahr-West Art Museum, housed in a magnificent Victorian mansion. This museum features an eclectic collection ranging from classic to contemporary art, including works by Picasso and Andy Warhol. Probably the museum's biggest claim to fame is the creation of the annual quirky **Sputnikfest**, drawing visitors from all over to celebrate the landing of part of the Russian spacecraft, Sputnik IV, in 1961. If you cannot make it to the festival, you can view the very spot it landed by a marker on 8th street in front of the museum.

610 North 8th Street

manitowoc.org/1006/Rahr-West-Art-Museum

West of The Lake Gardens

Stroll through the serene beauty of West of the Lake Gardens, a six acre botanical paradise overlooking Lake Michigan. These meticulously maintained gardens feature a dazzling array of flower beds, tranquil ponds, and artful sculptures. The garden's layout provides a peaceful retreat and a feast for the eyes with vibrant colors and intricate landscape designs. The gardens are open from the end of May to October.

915 Memorial Drive

westfoundation.us

Mariner's Trail

Experience the breathtaking views along Mariners Trail, a scenic pathway that stretches seven miles between Manitowoc and Two Rivers along the shore of Lake Michigan. This well-maintained trail is perfect for biking, walking, or jogging, with many access points and resting spots that offer spectacular vistas of the lake. Art installations and beautifully landscaped gardens along the route enhance the visual experience.

marinerstrail.net

Henry Schuette Park

Explore the expansive Henry Schuette Park, covering over 65 acres and offering a plethora of recreational activities. The lower part of the park is nature at its best. There's an accessible kayak launch, fitness zone, and six miles of walking trails that wind through wooded areas and open spaces. The Ice Age Trail makes its way through this section of the park. The upper portion has a playground and shelters.

3800 Broadway Street

manitowoc.org

Take A Cruise On The SS Badger

The SS Badger Car Ferry is not only a functional means of transportation but also a historic and iconic feature of Manitowoc. This legendary ferry offers a unique way to travel across Lake Michigan, connecting Manitowoc, Wisconsin, to Ludington, Michigan. The SS Badger is the largest car ferry ever to sail Lake Michigan and is designated as a National Historic Landmark. More than just a boat ride, a journey on the SS Badger includes access to amenities such as a movie lounge, a gift shop, a café, and spacious outdoor decks for enjoying the panoramic views of the lake. The voyage itself makes for a relaxing and scenic 4-hour trip, providing a memorable experience whether you're crossing for fun, as part of a trip, or merely to enjoy the ride on a piece of floating history.

900 South Lakeview Drive

ssbadger.com

Take a ride across Lake Michigan on the Badger

Celebrate The Evergleam Aluminum Christmas Tree

Manitowoc was once the home of the leading manufacturers of aluminum goods. One of the most popular products was the Evergleam aluminum Christmas tree by the Aluminum Specialty Company in the 1960s and 70s. Every year, the city celebrates these shiny creations with 'Evergleam on 8th', a seasonal event where downtown businesses display these trees during the holidays. There are trolley rides and a walking tour you can take for a fee.

Downtown Manitowoc Thanksgiving through the holidays

evergleams.org

Things To Do Around Manitowoc

Pinecrest Historical Village

Step back in time at Pinecrest Historical Village, a captivating outdoor museum that offers a glimpse into the rural life of Manitowoc County from the 1840s to the early 20th century. Spread over 60 acres, the village features more than 25 historic buildings, including a schoolhouse, a general store, a blacksmith shop, and a church, all authentically furnished to reflect their respective eras. Interactive exhibits and live demonstrations, such as blacksmithing and butter churning, provide a hands-on historical experience that engages both children and adults. It's not just a visit; it's an immersive journey into the past.

924 Pinecrest Road

manitowochistory.org

Farm Wisconsin Discovery Center

Engage with agricultural heritage at the Farm Wisconsin Discovery Center, between Manitowoc and Sheboygan, an educational facility dedicated to promoting the understanding of the state's farming and rural life. The center offers a range of interactive exhibits, educational programs, and hands-on activities that focus on agriculture, sustainability, and the food chain. Visitors can take part in animal feeding sessions, and viewing (if you're lucky) the birth of a calf. I absolutely love the **Wisconsin Cafe,** an indoor cafe in which the chef comes up with creative breakfast and lunch options. There's also a gift shop and visitor information.

7001 Gass Lake Road

farmwisconsin.org

Henning's Wisconsin Cheese

Sure, I'm a little partial to my nearest local cheesemaker, but that's for good reason. The cheesemakers at this rural Kiel factory consistently win national and world cheesemaking awards. This family-owned cheese factory is a half-hour drive from Manitowoc. Trust me, the fresh cheese curds are worth the drive alone. Henning's offers a unique experience where visitors can watch cheese being made through large viewing windows, explore the history of cheesemaking in their museum, and taste a variety of cheeses, including their famous cheddar wheels and specialty curds. The on-site store also allows you to purchase fresh cheeses and other local delicacies. It's a delightful exploration of Wisconsin's dairy culture, appealing to cheese lovers of all ages.

20201 Point Creek Road, Kiel

henningscheese.com

Shopping

Pine River Dairy

This rural dairy has a nice store where you can purchase cheese, candy, coffee, and local sausage. Besides the cheese, what the locals really love about this place is the 25 cent ice cream cones.

10115 English Lake Road

pineriverdairy.com

Dr. Freud's Records & Tapes

Immerse yourself in a world of vintage vinyl at Dr. Freud's Records & Tapes. This specialty shop is a treasure trove for music enthusiasts looking for rare records, classic cassettes, and unique tapes. Dr. Freud's offers knowledgeable staff who share your passion for music and can help you find that perfect album to complete your collection or start a new one.

925 South 8th Street

Phone: (920) 684-6700

The Granary Boutique

This women's boutique has a wide selection of women's fashionable clothing and accessories with sizes up to 3X.

206 North 8th Street

shopthegranary.com

Pink Petal Boutique

This adorable women's boutique offers fresh up-to-date fashion. Tops, dresses, and everything in between, including fun accessories at affordable prices. Size small to x-large.

912 South 8th Street

pinkpetalboutiquellc.com

The Mad Hatter

Come and explore the eclectic and "scary" offerings at The Mad Hatter, a unique store that celebrates Halloween every day. Shop here for items you cannot find anywhere else.

901 South 8th Street

deadbydawn.com

LaDeDa Books & Beans

Delve into the literary world at LaDeDa Books & Beans, a cozy bookstore where you can grab a coffee or smoothie. This shop offers a wide selection of books, from the latest bestsellers to rare finds and local authors. Frequent literary events, book signings, and reading groups invite community engagement, making LaDeDa a cultural hub in Manitowoc.

1624 New York Avenue

ladedabooksblog.blogspot.com

Graced Boutique

Step into Graced Boutique for a stylish and contemporary shopping experience. This boutique features a carefully curated selection of women's clothing, accessories, and beauty products that reflect the latest fashion trends.

914 South 8th Street

gracedco.com

Places to eat and drink in Manitowoc

Coffee and Bakery

Retro 8th Coffee & Acai

Retro 8th Coffee & Acai stands out with its vibrant, retro-inspired décor and a menu that's just as lively and colorful. Specializing in both traditional coffee options and more exotic choices like acai bowls and smoothies, this spot is a hit among those looking for a nutritious and tasty option.

801 North 8th Street

Phone: (920) 374-6302

PK's Beans N' Cream

PK's Beans N' Cream combines the coziness of a neighborhood coffee shop with the indulgence of an ice cream parlor. This unique establishment offers a wide range of coffee drinks, from espressos to lattes, all complemented by delicious Cedar Crest ice cream.

908 North 8th Street

Phone: (920) 682-9980

Jenn's Java

Jenn's Java is renowned for its strong community vibe and exceptional coffee. This local favorite prides itself on its artisanal approach to coffee making, featuring a menu of classic and specialty beverages made from high-quality, locally sourced coffee beans. The warm, inviting atmosphere makes Jenn's Java a perfect spot for catching up with friends or enjoying a quiet moment alone with a book and a perfectly brewed cup.

1124 Washington Street

Phone: (920) 682-8804

Hartman's Bakery

Hartman's Bakery is a traditional bakery that has been serving Manitowoc for generations. Known for its wide variety of baked goods, Hartman's excels in everything from fresh bread and rolls to custom cakes and sweet pastries. This bakery is famous for its doughnuts, which are considered some of the best in the area.

901 North 11th Street

hartmansbakery.com

Bakery On State

Bakery On State offers classic bakery items, crafting everything from artisan breads to gourmet cookies and pastries. Their focus on quality ingredients and sophisticated flavors caters to a discerning palate, making it a must-visit for anyone who appreciates fine baked goods.

436 North 9th Street

Phone: (920) 684-3650

Restaurants

Wrap It Up

Wrap It Up serves healthy breakfast and lunch options like omelets, panini, and hot and cold wraps. You can also get vegetarian options. There's an inside counter and table seating. Also serving Colectivo coffee.

830 South 8th Street

Late's

Late's is a Manitowoc classic offering burgers, breakfast, and broasted chicken. It has diner vibes with counter seating available.

1924 South 18th Street

Phone: (920) 682-1539

Courthouse Pub

Courthouse Pub is a local staple known for its microbrewery and scrumptious American cuisine. The pub offers a warm, inviting atmosphere where diners can enjoy a range of dishes made from locally sourced ingredients. Their menu features everything from gourmet burgers and fresh seafood to a variety of craft beers brewed on-site. It's a perfect spot for a casual meal in a friendly setting. I'm gonna give a shout out to the pub's cheese curds. They're delicious and made with Henning's curds.

1001 South 8th Street

courthousepub.com

Ryan's On York

Ryan's on York is a trendy gastropub known for its sophisticated menu and chic atmosphere. This dining spot features a variety of craft beers, artisan cocktails, and an innovative menu that includes gourmet burgers, creative handhelds, and artisanal appetizers.

712 York Street

ryansonyork.com

Brick's Bar and Grill

The specialty at Brick's is burgers. Not just any burgers, these are tantalizing gourmet style burgers. Try 'Brick's and Mortar', a third pound of beef, smothered in bourbon cheese dip and piled with fried haystack onion. It's delicious.

939 South 8th Street

bricksmanitowoc.com

Bars, Wineries, and Breweries

PetSkull Brewing Co

PetSkull Brewing Company is a popular spot in the heart of Manitowoc's revitalized downtown area. This vibrant microbrewery prides itself on a rotating selection of handcrafted beers, brewed right on site. With a cozy taproom atmosphere, PetSkull offers a welcoming environment to enjoy unique brews ranging from classic ales and lagers to adventurous IPAs and stouts. They often feature live music and local food trucks, making it a hub of activity and a favorite gathering place for the community.

1015 Buffalo Street

petskullbrewing.com

Sabbatical Brewing Co

Sabbatical Brewing Co. is another excellent addition to Manitowoc's brewery scene, known for its innovative approach to craft beer. The brewery offers a wide range of beers with a focus on quality and creativity, ensuring there's always something new to try. The taproom is designed for comfort and conversation, featuring a laid-back vibe that's perfect for relaxing after a long day or catching up with friends over a pint of exceptional beer.

835 South 29th Street

sabbaticalbrewingco.com

Time Out Sports Bar & Grill

Time Out Sports Bar & Grill isn't just a place to catch the game; it's a venue that offers a wide selection of beers and spirits in a lively sports-focused atmosphere. With plenty of screens to watch your favorite sports, a menu filled with satisfying pub grub, and a fully stocked bar, it's a local favorite for a fun night out.

1027 North Rapids Road

timeoutsportsbarandgrill.net

Waterfront Wine Bar

Taking a break from all that beer, here's one for the wine fans. Waterfront Wine Bar has the perfect setting to enjoy an old-fashioned flight, craft cocktail, or sample wines and spirits from the dispensing machines. Have no fear beer lovers, you can get one of those too. For me, I'll have a Cotton Candy Moscato please.

2 North 8th Street

waterfrontwinebar.com

Sweet Treats

Beerntsen's Confectionary

Beerntsen's Confectionary offers a delightful blend of dining and history, serving as both an ice cream parlor, sandwich shop, and a candy shop. Known for its old-fashioned soda fountain and homemade chocolates, this eatery provides a nostalgic experience. This is a must-visit.

108 North 8th Street

beerntsens.com

Cedar Crest Ice Cream Parlor

What is probably the most instagrammable spot in Manitowoc? If you said Bernice, the Cedar Crest Guernsey, you'd probably be right. Bernice stands proud on 10th Street in front of the Cedar Crest Plant and Parlor, tempting people in passing cars to cool off with a satisfying scoop or two from the over 100 flavors of ice cream. This stop is a must for all ice cream fans. Just mention you're going to "the cow" and locals know exactly what you're talking about. (Photo page 123)

2000 South 10th Street

cedarcresticecream.com/our-parlor

Accommodations

Hotels and Bed and Breakfasts

Harbor Town Inn

Harbor Town Inn offers a comfortable and economical stay with a range of amenities designed for both leisure and business travelers. The hotel features spacious rooms, complimentary breakfast, an indoor pool, and a fitness center. Its location near Lake Michigan and various dining options makes it a convenient base for exploring Manitowoc and the surrounding areas.

4004 Calumet Avenue

harbortowninn.com

Inn On Maritime Bay-Ascend Hotel Collection

Inn On Maritime Bay is perfectly situated to offer guests stunning views of Lake Michigan. This hotel prides itself on its friendly service and comfortable rooms, which include options with a lake view. Amenities include an indoor pool, free Wi-Fi, and complimentary breakfast. It's an excellent choice for those who want to enjoy a relaxing waterfront stay while being close to downtown Manitowoc.

101 Maritime Drive

choicehotels.com

Dead by Dawn Dead & Breakfast

Dead by Dawn Dead & Breakfast offers an entirely unique experience, blending the charm of a traditional bed-and-breakfast with a spine-tingling twist that caters to lovers of horror and the macabre. Dead by Dawn Dead & Breakfast, housed in the beautifully restored historic building, features three guest rooms, each themed to evoke different eerie tales and creepy settings. It's known not just for its accommodations but also for its immersive experience, including frightfully themed breakfasts and interactions with ghostly characters. Ideal for those looking for something out of the ordinary. This B&B promises a stay filled with fun frights and spooky surprises.

901 South 8th Street

deadbydawn.com

Two Rivers

Welcome to Two Rivers, Wisconsin, a charming harbor town where the East and West Twin Rivers meet the majestic Lake Michigan. Known for its scenic beauty, rich maritime heritage, and the claim to fame as the birthplace of the iconic ice cream sundae, Two Rivers is a delightful destination for travelers seeking both relaxation and adventure.

Location

Two Rivers is just seven miles from downtown Manitowoc on Highway 42. The highway runs along the lakeshore at this point. If you are traveling on I-43, it takes about 19 minutes to get from the Highway 310 exit to Two Rivers.

Two Rivers Facts

- Two Rivers claims to be the birthplace of the ice cream sundae. In 1881, a local soda fountain owner, Edward Berners, allegedly concocted the first sundae when he drizzled chocolate syrup over vanilla ice cream at the request of a customer. This sweet invention quickly gained popularity, making Two Rivers a historical sweet spot.

- The town was the site of the Hamilton Manufacturing Company, established in the late 19th century, which became a leading producer of wood type used for printing newspapers and posters. This innovation helped revolutionize the printing industry and made Two Rivers a hub for industrial progress.

- Two Rivers was once a prominent location for tanneries that processed leather, contributing to Wisconsin's leather industry. This part of its industrial history highlights the town's role in broader economic activities beyond shipbuilding and printing.

- The population of Two Rivers is 11,166 (2022)

How Much Time To Spend In Two Rivers

You can get a nice overview of Two Rivers in a day visit, but if you want to take advantage of the beach, Point Beach State Park and other highlights, I would suggest a weekend.

Things To Do In Two Rivers

Two Rivers Highlights

Lighthouse

Two Rivers North Pier Lighthouse-This nearly all-wood structure was built in 1886. In 1968, it was taken out of service and moved to its present location in the Rogers Street Fishing Village. It remains one of the few Great Lake wooden structures still standing.

2102 Jackson Street

rogersstreet.com

Rawley Point Lighthouse-This lighthouse once marked the Chicago River in Chicago. In 1893, it was dismantled and shipped to Wisconsin to serve as the lighthouse at Rawley Point behind the keeper's house. In 1979, it was automated by the Coast Guard and it's still used as housing. The grounds are closed to the public, but visitors can view the lighthouse from Point Beach State Forest.

us-lighthouses.com/rawley-point-lighthouse

Hamilton Wood Type & Printing Museum

Art and history intersect at the Hamilton Wood Type & Printing Museum, where visitors can delve into the fascinating world of printing history and see the largest collection of wood type in the nation. This unique museum highlights Two Rivers' contributions to the American printing industry and offers hands-on workshops, making it a must-visit for history buffs and creative spirits alike. (Photo page 123)

1816 10th Street

woodtype.org

Neshotah Beach

Neshotah Beach is a beautiful sandy beach that offers a variety of outdoor activities. With volleyball courts, a beach house, picnic areas, and stunning views of Lake Michigan, it's perfect for a family day out or a relaxing time by the water.

2111 Pierce Street

Rogers Street Fishing Village

Dive into the local maritime history at this historic fishing village and museum. It features exhibits on the Great Lakes fishing industry, historic fishing boats, and the U.S. Life-Saving Service, providing a detailed look at the town's fishing heritage.

2102 Jackson Street

rogersstreet.com

Point Beach State Forest

For those who love the outdoors, Point Beach State Forest offers 3,000 acres of land with six miles of Lake Michigan shoreline. In the summer, this park is full of campers, hikers and beach goers. There are four trails, including the Ice Age National Scenic Trail, which runs for five miles inside the forest.

9400 County Road O

dnr.wisconsin.gov/topic/parks/pointbeach

Woodland Dunes Nature Center and Preserve

This nature preserve spans over 1,500 acres and features diverse habitats, including forests, prairies, and wetlands. It's a perfect spot for birdwatching, hiking, and experiencing the area's natural beauty.

3000 Hawthorne Avenue

woodlanddunes.org

The Washington House Museum & Visitors Center

Visit this historic site where the first ice cream sundae was reportedly served. Today, it serves as a museum showcasing local history, with a soda fountain and sundaes still available for guests.

1622 Jefferson Street

tworivers-history.org

Shopping

Schroeder's Department Store

The family-owned department store is a dying business, but in Two Rivers, Schroeder's Department Store has been in business since 1891. Schroeder's offers a wide variety of merchandise from unique gifts to home decorations, clothing, and more, all in a charming old-world atmosphere. When you're finished shopping, enjoy a coffee in the **Red Bank Coffeehouse**.

1623 Washington Street

schroederstore.com

The Read Apple Toy Shop

Stop in here if you're looking for toys, games, or books for the kiddos. The Read Apple has a wide selection of items to promote learning in infants to grade school-age children.

1623 Washington Street

thereadapple.com

Paper Crane Bookstore

Independent bookstores are one of the first places I visit when traveling to a new destination. Paper Crane Bookstore is that place in Two Rivers. Started by book lover Rebecca Crane and her husband after losing her job in tech, they opened the bookstore in 2023.

1610 Washington Street

papercranebookstore.com

Places to eat and drink in Two Rivers

Coffee and Bakery

The Hi Lift

Hi Lift is a vibrant café known for its excellent coffee and welcoming community atmosphere. Young owner Emilee Rysticken and her father converted the old Peterson Mobile Service Station and created a space for everyone in the community to gather. You can order on the website and pick up at the drive-through. I prefer going inside and enjoying the atmosphere. They also offer baked goods for sale.

1207 Madison Street

Highlift.square.site

Christina's Cakery & Baked Goods

Get your baked goods here, including donuts, pastries, and cakes. Make sure you go early for the best selection. Christina's often sells out of certain items. Of course, you can always call ahead for an order.

1213 Madison Street

Phone: (920) 794-7244

Restaurants

Kurtz's Pub & Deli

Kurtz's has been around forever. It's nostalgic for me because once upon a time, they used to serve drinks in giant punch bowls and a group of us would go there and sip these exotic drinks while sitting around a table and enjoying a great conversation.

Not much has changed (except those giant punch bowl drinks). This traditional German pub and deli serves a selection of German and other European imported beers. The menu offers a wide variety of food from wraps and classic hot and cold sandwiches. They have daily specials and peel and eat shrimp on Fridays.

1410 Washington Street

Phone: (920) 793-1222

Port Sandy Bay

Port Sandy Bay has a fun claim to fame. It's home to the Sno-Coaster pizza. Whatever is that you ask? This restaurant took their pizza size one step further by offering their pizza on an old-fashioned aluminum Sno-Coaster sled. That's a 20 inch pizza! Oh, and the pizza is delish. If pizza doesn't entice you, you can get the standard burger and chicken sandwich. Fish Fry is available Wednesday, Thursday, and Friday.

6421 Highway O

Phone: (920) 793-2345

Bars, Wine, and Breweries

Cool City Brewing

Don't let the name fool you. Cool City is also a coffee and breakfast place, an amazing restaurant, and a brewpub. So technically, it should be listed in all of the eat and drink categories. Since brewing was in the name, it's listed here.

Cool City Brewing has revitalized the entire downtown area of Two Rivers. It's a unique gathering place that has a cool industrial vibe with plenty of space. There's a vast selection of their own beers, an extensive menu of full sized drink flights, and tasty food choices. I can recommend trying the 'T'Rivers Cheese Curd Flight' for starters and a 'Cool City Smashburger' (mushrooms and Swiss for me). (Photo page 123)

1718 West Park Street

coolcitybrewing.com

Sweet Treats

Scream 'N Conuts

Remember Emilee Rystricken from Hi Lift, the cafe I mentioned above? Well, she has another business in Two Rivers. Scream 'N Conuts is the ice cream shop she started when she was just 17 years old. Ice cream here is served the traditional way, but also inside a so-called 'conut'. Inspired by a "chimney cake", a round cylinder of sweet dough that she saw on a trip to Prague, she fills her conut with ice cream. You can't miss this place. It's the pink building you see driving into Two Rivers from Manitowoc. Open May through the summer.

1200 Washington Street

screamnconuts.com

Accommodations

Hotels and Bed and Breakfast

Lighthouse Inn

The only Two Rivers hotel directly on the beautiful shores of Lake Michigan, the Lighthouse Inn offers breathtaking views. Guests can enjoy an on-site restaurant with lake views, a heated indoor pool, and a variety of room types to accommodate any travel need.

1515 Memorial Drive

lhinn.com

Village Inn On The Lake

Overlooking Lake Michigan, Village Inn on the Lake features poolside, lakeside, and woodside rooms, plus a 24 full hookups RV park and camp store, indoor heated pool and hot tub, and bicycle rentals. It's conveniently located across Memorial Drive and the Mariners Trail and has great access to Two Rivers and Manitowoc.

3310 Memorial Drive

villigeinnwi.com

Red Forest Bed and Breakfast Inn

Red Forest Bed and Breakfast combines historic charm with modern comforts. This elegant B&B offers a cozy stay with gourmet breakfasts, beautifully decorated rooms, and personalized service, making it ideal for a romantic getaway or a peaceful retreat.

1421 25th Street

redforestbb.com

Campgrounds

Point Beach State Forest

Point Beach State Forest offers over 3,000 acres of land along six miles of pristine Lake Michigan shoreline. It features 127 well-maintained wooded campsites suitable for both tents and RVs, hiking trails (including a segment of the Ice Age Trail), a historic lighthouse, and biking paths. Seventy campsites offer electric hookup. It's an ideal spot for nature lovers and outdoor enthusiasts seeking a peaceful retreat amidst beautiful surroundings.

9400 County Highway O

dnr.wisconsin.gov/topic/parks/pointbeach/info

Kewaunee

Kewaunee is one of our smaller Wisconsin Harbor Towns. Imagine a place where the charm of small-town America blends seamlessly with the majesty of natural landscapes, where the lapping waves of Lake Michigan beckon, and the history is as rich as the soil in its vibrant farmlands. Welcome to Kewaunee, lying along the picturesque shores of Lake Michigan, offering an idyllic retreat for travelers seeking both tranquility and adventure.

Location

Kewaunee is about 20 miles north of Two Rivers and about 10 miles south of Algoma.

Kewaunee Facts

- Native American tribes originally inhabited the area around Kewaunee, including the Potawatomi and Menominee, who used the rich resources of the region for hunting, fishing, and trade.

- In the early 1830s, European settlers, primarily of Belgian, German, and Czech descent, established communities in the area. Kewaunee's architecture, traditions, and culture today reflect the influence of these settlers.

- Because of its location on Lake Michigan, Kewaunee grew as an important maritime center in the late 19th and early 20th centuries, with shipbuilding, commercial fishing, and port activities playing vital roles in its economy.

- The railroad boom in the late 19th century connected Kewaunee to larger markets, promoting its growth as an industrial hub, especially in the lumber and agriculture sectors.

- There was once car ferry service between Kewaunee and Frankfort, Michigan

- Today, while still proud of its maritime and industrial heritage, Kewaunee has evolved into a popular tourist destination, drawing visitors with its historical sites, natural beauty, and lakeside activities.

- The population of Kewaunee is 2,787 (2021)

How Much Time To Spend In Kewaunee

Take your time and explore Kewaunee easily on a weekend, or stop in for a day. Kewaunee may not be a large city, but there are some things you need to check out.

Things To Do In Kewaunee

Like all the Wisconsin Harbor Towns, Lake Michigan plays a major role in bringing people to the area. Sport fishing is a spotlight and there are many Lake Michigan charters for hire here.

Kewaunee Highlights

Lighthouses

Pierhead Lighthouse- Visitors to the Kewaunee Pierhead Lighthouse can bask in the picturesque scenery that this iconic structure affords. At the end of the pier, it's an ideal spot for a leisurely walk with the symphony of Lake Michigan's waves accompanying your steps. The lighthouse itself is a popular subject for photographers and a symbol of the town's nautical heritage. The lighthouse is open for occasional tours during the summer months. Please watch the website for more information.

kewauneepierheadlighthouse.org

World's Tallest Grandfather Clock

Sitting at a towering 35 feet 10 inches, this iconic Kewaunee landmark almost disappeared from the landscape of the city after a decade of disrepair. Thank goodness a local citizen began a campaign to move the clock from its original location and have it rebuilt and back to working order. The community raised more than $30,000 to give the clock a new life in its current home. It proudly sits at the trailhead of the Ahnapee State Trail in downtown Kewaunee.

Ahnapee State Trail

At 44 miles long, the Ahnapee Trail begins in Kewaunee and continues north to Sturgeon Bay. A part of the converted rails-to-trails system, the wide trail is paved with a limestone surface, making it easy to navigate. Users enjoy the trail year-round, used primarily by snowmobilers in winter, although you can cross-country ski on it.

ahnapeestatetrail.com

Bruemmer Park Zoo

In the heart of Kewaunee County, the Bruemmer Park Zoo occupies a modest but beautifully maintained space within the larger Bruemmer Park. It's a favorite spot for both locals and visitors. While it's not as large as many urban zoos, Bruemmer Park Zoo houses a variety of animals, many of which are native to the region. Visitors can expect to see animals such as deer, peafowl, goats, and more. The exhibits aim to provide naturalistic environments for its animals, emphasizing their comfort and well-being.

E4280 County Road F

bruemmerparkzoo.com

Tug Ludington

During the summer months, you can tour this piece of World War II history. This vessel was built in Oyster Bay, New York and was specifically made to help during the war. Its role was to tow ammunition barges across the English Channel to Normandy. The Tug Ludington even took part in D-Day. After the war, it returned to the US, getting transferred to Kewaunee in 1947. Tug Ludington may have retired from wartime duties, but it still found a useful second life helping in the construction of many harbors.

There is a small fee to tour the Tug Ludington at its resting place in Harbor Park.

kewaunee.org/tug-ludington

Shopping

Wakker's Cheese

Specializing in gouda cheese, Wakker's Cheese showcases Dutch recipes and other cheese and imported sweets. Family-run, the owner is fabulous. Cheese is shipped across the nation from this location.

409 Milwaukee Street

www.wakkercheese.com

Lafond's Fish Market

Local fish market that features freshly caught whitefish and more. People rave about the smoked salmon. The fish comes in daily from local fishermen. Try the brown sugar smoked salmon.

216 Milwaukee Street

Pretty Please Boutique

Quality women's and children's clothing and accessories at reasonable prices. Sizes small to 3X.

222 Ellis Street

prettypleasekewaunee.com

Places to eat and drink In Kewaunee

Coffee and Bakery

The Bakery Bar

Not only is there coffee and fresh bakery here, but also a small lunch menu. Down-home, welcoming atmosphere. Stop in for a coffee or even a Bloody Mary.

408 Milwaukee Street

Restaurants

Anchor Down Family Restaurant

Your classic Wisconsin family restaurant. Nothing fancy, just great down-home food. Burgers, lunch plates, and substantial breakfasts. Open for breakfast and lunch only

301 Ellis Street

Waterfront Bar and Grill

Serving American style food, pizza, burgers, wings, and a Friday Fish Fry that Wisconsin is famous for. There's a full bar and live music in the summer.

215 North Main street

waterfrontbarandgrillkewaunee.com

Gibs On The Lake

Supper Club and steakhouse on the lake. Excellent menu choices such as pasta, prime rib, and scallops. On Wednesdays and Thursdays, it offers traditional German dishes like schnitzel and sauerbraten.

N110 State Highway 42

gibsonthelake.com

Sweet Treats

Kewaunee Custard and Grill

Best place to grab a frozen custard on a hot day. Offering flavors of the day, specialty sundaes and shakes. A basic burger menu is also offered if you want a full meal.

707 Main Street

kewauneecustard.com

Accommodations

Hotels

Harbor Lights Lodge

This is a no-nonsense hotel right near the water and marina. Splendid views of the lake in the lakeside rooms. Free Wi-Fi access and free parking.

211 Milwaukee Street

harborlightlodge.com

Campgrounds

Kewaunee RV & Campground

Nice campground just out of town with four cabins, swimming pool, full hookups and water and electric sites, laundry facilities and more. There are a lot of seasonal sites here too. Open seasonally.

333 Terraqua Drive

kewauneerv.com

Algoma

Algoma is a quaint harbor town that promises visitors a unique blend of natural beauty, history, and Midwestern hospitality. Known for its fishing heritage, vibrant downtown murals, and proximity to Door County, Algoma is an ideal destination for those looking to escape the hustle and bustle of city life. With it being so close to Door County, you can make this a quiet home base for a low key Door County vacation. Whether you're an outdoor enthusiast, history buff, or a foodie, you can find your own slice of heaven along Lake Michigan right here.

Location

Algoma is situated about 12 miles north of Kewaunee, 32 miles southeast of Green Bay, and 17 miles south of Sturgeon Bay. Highway 42 is the main highway that runs through Algoma.

City Facts

- Founded on timber and shipbuilding: Algoma's early economy was heavily reliant on its timber and shipbuilding industries. The town was originally called "Ahnapee," which was eventually changed to Algoma in 1897, a name believed to be derived from an Indian term for "park of flowers."

- **An Early Native American Settlement:** Before European settlers arrived, the area that is now Algoma was home to various Native American tribes. The Menominee tribe, in particular, had a significant presence in the region, utilizing the fertile land and rich fishing waters of Lake Michigan.

- **The Great Fire of 1871:** Algoma was one of the many communities affected by the Great Fire of 1871, also known as the Peshtigo Fire, which is considered one of the most devastating forest fires ever to occur in North America.

- **Home to Wisconsin's Oldest Winery:** Algoma is the proud location of von Stiehl Winery, Wisconsin's oldest licensed winery, which was established in 1967. The winery resides in a Civil War-era building and is known for its wide array of wines that include traditional varietals and fruit wines made from local produce.

- Today the population of Algoma is 3,219 (2021)

How Much Time To Spend

As I mentioned in the introduction, Algoma makes a great home base for a Door County vacation. You may not be in the thick of things here, but many enjoy its quiet charm compared to the tourist influx of Door County. If you choose that, give yourself a week. If you intend to spend most of your time in Algoma, a weekend is ideal.

Things To Do In Algoma

Algoma Highlights

Algoma Lighthouse

The Algoma Pierhead Lighthouse, with its distinctive red hue, is a beacon for the community. Though it is not open to the public for tours, its presence is a historical emblem and it provides an idyllic backdrop for photos. You cannot walk right up to it, but you can walk the piers on either side.

1 Steele Street

lighthousefriends.com/light.asp?ID=254

Algoma Mural and Historical Self-Guided Walk

My number one personal favorite is the Historic Algoma Walking Tour. Algoma's downtown area is adorned with vibrant murals that capture the spirit of the community and its heritage. These public artworks tell stories of the town's history, its connection to the water, and the natural beauty of the region. Along with the murals, you will discover places of historical significance like the Hotel Stebbins. Visitors can take a self-guided tour. You can use the link below to find and download the guide with explanations of everything included on the walk. (Photo page 180)

Various spots downtown

visitalgomawi.com/art

Crescent Beach and Boardwalk

Crescent Beach is the city's main beach area. It offers a pristine shoreline ideal for picnics, sunbathing, and swimming in the warmer months. The adjoining boardwalk provides a scenic route for walkers and joggers, with benches strategically placed for those who want to pause and soak in the views of Lake Michigan. It runs a half mile from the Visitors Center to the marina. Visitors can expect a clean, well-maintained sandy beach, clear waters and a newer changing house. The boardwalk is ADA accessible for all ages and offers an excellent vantage point for sunrise views.

Lake Street

friendsofcrescentbeach.org

Kayaking the Ahnapee River

Algoma is a great place to get out on the water. You can kayak on the Ahnapee River by launching from Olsen Park. Kayaking the river is great for beginners and those looking for a leisurely paddle. You can also launch from Crescent Beach and paddle near the Lake Michigan shoreline. Just beware of the winds and lake current. If you don't have your own kayak or other watercraft, no worries, you can rent them from Bayshore Outfitters (rental site near the 2nd Street bridge), or some local campgrounds.

Ahnapee State Trail

This 48-mile rail trail runs through Algoma. Used by hikers, bikers, runners, and cross-country skiers, the crushed limestone surface is relatively flat and travels through a variety of landscapes. The main trailhead is located off 6th Street in Algoma, with other parking areas available in the area.

dnr.wisconsin.gov/topic/parks/ahnapee/info

Fishing

Fishing is a way of life in Algoma. It's a year-round sport. In summer, take one of several fishing charters out into Lake Michigan and catch that prized salmon or trout. In winter, head to the Ahnapee River for trout and pike. You can find a list of charters on the website listed below.

fishingbooker.com/destinations/location/us/WI/algoma

Shopping

Bay Shore Outfitters

Bay Shore Outfitters is your go-to destination for outdoor gear and apparel in Algoma. Specializing in kayaking and stand-up paddle boarding (SUP), they provide everything you need for an adventure on the water. They also rent kayaks, paddle boards, and more at the 2nd Street Bridge location.

219 State Street

bayshoreoutfitters.com/algoma

Fishline Studios

A gallery and creative space, Fishline Studios is a showcase of local art and craftsmanship, featuring the works of regional artists. It's an ideal stop for visitors who are interested in taking home a piece of Algoma's art scene. You can reserve time at the studio to let your imagination run wild and create your own art. Take a spin at the potter's wheel. One of the coolest things is that if you would like to host a small class for others, you can rent the studio, charge your students, and keep that fee.

213 Steele Street

fishlinestudios.com

2nd Hand Rose

2nd Hand Rose is a beloved local second-hand store offering an array of items from clothing to household goods. It's perfect for treasure hunters and bargain shoppers. Visitors can explore a wide range of products like vintage clothes, second-hand books, used furniture, and unique home decor. It's a place where each visit brings a new discovery.

423 4th Street

Places To Eat And Drink In Algoma

Coffee and Bakery

Caffe Tlazo

Caffé Tlazo is an inviting coffeehouse known for its quality coffees, teas, and Mediterranean-inspired menu. It's a popular spot for both locals and visitors to relax and savor a warm beverage. Guests can expect a variety of coffee options from classic espressos to lattes, along with a selection of teas. Bakery items include pastries and light breakfast options, perfect for starting the day or enjoying a mid-afternoon treat.

607 4th St

caffetlazo.com

Northwater Bakery and Deli

Northwater Bakery and Deli rides piggyback with the Captain's Galley Room, which is a full-service restaurant. The bakery and deli also have a menu consisting primarily of sandwiches and salads for breakfast and lunch. There is also a delectable bakery case, and this is where you can order those specialized cakes by JoAnn.

133 North Water Street

northwaterbakeryanddeli.com

Restaurants

Son Of Skaliwags

Don't let the unassuming dive bar facade fool you. What Chef Marshall creates behind the bar for all to see is extraordinary. Skaliwags is a high-end dining experience that prides itself on serving "five-star food in a little dive bar." It's a place in which culinary finesse meets a relaxed atmosphere. The restaurant prides itself on serving only the finest seafood and cuts of meat. It's typically a busy place, so get there early.

312 Clark Street

sonofskaliwags.com

Captain's Galley Room

This popular cafe serves breakfast and lunch during the week and a breakfast menu on weekends. Visitors will find a menu filled with comfort food classics, hearty breakfasts, and daily specials that reflect the local taste. If you want more than just the bakery and deli options that North Water Bakery and Deli offer, try Captain's Galley.

133 North water Street

northwaterbakeryanddeli.com

Three Eleven Bar and Bistro

I love the bistro setting in this newcomer to Algoma. The menu includes a lobster roll and a fabulous mushroom burger smothered in garlic aioli. Entrees feature the classic Beef Bourguignon and Pan Seared Salmon.

311 Steele Street

threeelevenbarbistro.com

Bars, Wine, and Breweries

Von Stiehl Winery

Wisconsin's oldest licensed winery, von Stiehl offers more than just wine tastings – their on-site shop provides a range of wines for purchase, wine-related accessories, and gourmet food items. Try the original Cherry Bounce, made from Door County cherries. Their wines are distributed throughout the state. After you're finished with the wine, head next door and check out the cidery.

115 Navarino Street

vonstiehl.com

Ahnapee Brewery

Located just a stone's throw from the shores of Lake Michigan, Ahnapee Brewery offers a range of craft beers in a cozy, rustic taproom setting. The brewery originally started in the 1860s and was revived in 2013, continuing a long tradition of brewing in Algoma. Beer enthusiasts can enjoy a variety of brews that span from traditional styles to more experimental flavors. The taproom provides a welcoming environment with a friendly community vibe. They have small bites available, but also welcome you to bring in food from local stores and restaurants. Hands down, my favorite brew is the classic Two Stall, named after its original Algoma location.

202 Clark Street

ahnapeebrewery.com

Sweet Treats

Sweets and Other Stuff

Of course, Algoma has a candy shop! Not only that, the shop carries popcorn, and like the name suggests, "other stuff". Sweets and Other Stuff is open seasonally, so make sure you find the store on Facebook for more information. It's located in one of my favorite buildings in Algoma. Look for the flying mermaid above the door.

522 4th Street

Accommodations

Hotels and Bed and Breakfast

Hotel Stebbins

Hotel Stebbins, an Algoma landmark, combines historic charm with modern amenities and has an on-site restaurant and bar that's popular with locals and visitors alike. Guests will find comfortable accommodations and can choose from a range of rooms, including some with views of the lake. The hotel's restaurant serves a variety of dishes and is known for its Friday Fish Fry.

201 Steele Street

.thehotelstebbins.com

Algoma Beach Hotel

The Algoma Beach Motel offers a scenic lakefront stay, with many rooms providing panoramic views of Lake Michigan. It's a family-friendly location with easy access to the beach for a stroll or a picnic. The motel features amenities that include free Wi-Fi, complimentary breakfast during peak season, grills for a cookout, and a variety of room types to suit different group sizes.

1500 Lake Street

algomabeachmotel.com

At The Waters Edge B&B

This B&B offers a serene retreat on the edge of Lake Michigan. It's designed with relaxation in mind, featuring gardens and a private beach. Visitors will be treated to elegantly decorated rooms, each with unique themes and a full homemade breakfast. It's an ideal spot for a romantic getaway or a peaceful solo escape.

N7136 State Highway 42

atthewatersedgebnb.com

Campgrounds

Ahnapee Shores Camping Resort

Ahnapee Shores Campground is a family-operated facility that offers visitors a peaceful camping experience near the banks of the Ahnapee River. It is well-suited for both long-term stays and weekend getaways. This campground features spacious sites for RVs with full hookups, including water, sewer, and electric. Tent camping spots are also available. Guests can enjoy fishing in the river, kayaking, and easy access to the Ahnapee State Trail for walking and biking.

E6053 West Wilson Road

ahnapee.com

Timber Trail Campground

Located in a tranquil wooded area, Timber Trail Campground is designed for those looking to immerse themselves in nature. It's a short drive from Algoma, providing a rustic camping experience with modern conveniences. The campground has a variety of campsites, including options with electric hookups. Amenities include a camp store, playground, heated pool, and shower facilities. Timber Trail is an excellent choice for families and outdoor enthusiasts who want a base to explore the surrounding nature preserves and Lake Michigan's coastline.

N8326 Co Road M

timbertrailcampgrounds.com

Sturgeon Bay

Sandwiched between Lake Michigan and the Bay of Green Bay, Sturgeon Bay is the picturesque gateway to Door County and the county's largest city. This charming harbor town, a blend of rich history and contemporary allure, offers visitors a unique blend of natural beauty, historic architecture, and a vibrant arts scene. It's an ideal destination for those seeking a blend of maritime adventure, culinary delights, and tranquil relaxation.

Sturgeon Bay makes a great home base to explore all of Door County, with tons of things to do. I'll admit, I drove right through Sturgeon Bay, making a beeline for points north in Door County more often than I should admit. After spending a few days just exploring Sturgeon Bay, I came to a new appreciation of the downtown area and the many other charms located here.

Location

Sturgeon Bay is in Door County, Wisconsin, acting as a natural divider between the bay of Green Bay and Lake Michigan. The town is uniquely positioned on a slim channel that not only provides stunning waterfront views but also a rich maritime heritage. It's about a 25 minute drive from Algoma on Highway 42 and a 45-minute drive northeast of Green Bay.

Sturgeon Bay Facts

- Sturgeon Bay's shipbuilding industry dates back to the 19th century. It became especially significant during World War II when local shipyards were critical in building vessels for the U.S. Navy, contributing significantly to the war effort.

- The arrival of the railroad in Sturgeon Bay in the late 1800s was a pivotal moment, transforming the town into a regional transportation hub. This development significantly boosted the local economy, particularly in industries like lumber and shipping.

- In the early 20th century, Door County, including Sturgeon Bay, experienced a boom in cherry production, becoming one of the largest producers of cherries in the United States. This period marked Sturgeon Bay as a major player in the agricultural sector.

- Sturgeon Bay is home to three lighthouses, including the Sherwood Point Lighthouse and the Sturgeon Bay Canal North Pierhead Light. These lighthouses have been guiding ships safely through the waters of Green Bay and Lake Michigan for over a century.

- The historic Teweles and Brandeis Granary, dating back to 1901, was a key structure in the city's agricultural past. It is one of, if not the only wooden granary left on the Great Lakes. In a remarkable feat of preservation, the structure is currently in Phase II of its preservation project.

- As of the latest census, Sturgeon Bay has a population of approximately 9,706 (2021) residents, embodying a close-knit community atmosphere.

How Much Time To Spend In Sturgeon Bay

I would suggest spending a long weekend in Sturgeon Bay for starters. If you want to make Sturgeon Bay your home base for visiting the entire Door County area, give yourself a week.

Things To Do In Sturgeon Bay

Sturgeon Bay Highlights

Lighthouses

Sturgeon Bay Ship Canal North Pierhead Lighthouse- This iconic red lighthouse, at the entrance of the Sturgeon Bay Ship Canal, played a crucial role in guiding ships safely through the hazardous waters of Lake Michigan to Green Bay. While the lighthouse itself is not open to the public for tours, you can walk out to it provided the weather conditions are right.

2501 Canal Road

sturgeonbay.net/plan/lighthouses

Sturgeon Bay Canal Light- This lighthouse is at the Coast Guard Station near the Pierhead Lighthouse. It is on the National Register of Historic Places. You can park at the station and walk to this lighthouse, but please watch the signs and stay off the private property.

2501 Canal Road

sturgeonbay.net/plan/lighthouses

Sherwood Point Lighthouse- Sherwood Point Lighthouse, established in 1883 and automated in 1983, making it the last manned lighthouse on the Great Lakes. Perched on a picturesque point overlooking the bay of Green Bay, it has been guiding mariners with its consistent light for over a century. Unlike the Canal

Lighthouse, Sherwood Point Lighthouse offers a more intimate glimpse into lighthouse living, as it is occasionally open to the public during special events and is also available for rent through the U.S. Coast Guard, a unique accommodation experience.

sturgeonbay.net/plan/lighthouses

Door County Maritime Museum

A must-visit for history and maritime enthusiasts, this museum offers insightful exhibits on the region's rich maritime history, including shipwrecks, lighthouses, and shipbuilding. It's a great place to learn about the area's nautical heritage.

120 North Madison Avenue

dcmm.org

Potawatomi State Park

Offering stunning views of Green Bay and a variety of outdoor activities like hiking, biking, and camping. The park's natural beauty and four extensive trails make it a perfect spot for nature lovers. You will find a two-point-eight mile segment and the Eastern Terminus of Wisconsin's 1200 mile Ice Age National Scenic Trail inside the park.

3740 County Highway PD

dnr.wisconsin.gov/topic/parks/potawatomi

Third Avenue Playworks

This intimate theater in downtown Sturgeon Bay hosts a variety of live performances, from plays and musicals to concerts and comedy shows. It's a great place to catch high-quality, local entertainment.

239 North 3rd Avenue

thirdavenueplayworks.org/

Crossroads At Big Creek

A 200 acre unique combination of nature preserve, learning center, and historical village, offering trails, educational programs, and a look into the area's past. It's a magnificent spot for both learning and recreation. The nature preserve and trails are open all the time. Leashed dogs are welcome on trails with the exception of the Cove Estuary Preserve.

2041 Michigan St

crossroadsatbigcreek.org

Take A Segway Tour Of Sturgeon Bay

A fun and unique way to explore Sturgeon Bay, these guided Segway tours offer a different perspective on the city's sights and history. The tour takes off at the Maritime Museum, and after a short driving lesson, crosses the bridge and gives you a rundown of historical sites and shipbuilding boatyards.

Phone: (920) 376-0256

glidenew.com/product/sturgeon-bay-canal-city-segway-tour

Graham Park

This charming waterfront park is a lovely spot for relaxation and recreation. Featuring beautiful landscaping, access to a two-and-a-half mile waterfront path, ping-pong tables, and a gazebo, it's a perfect place for a leisurely stroll, a picnic, or just to enjoy the outdoors. The park also hosts various community events throughout the year, making it a hub of local activity and a great place to experience the community spirit of Sturgeon Bay. People flock here in the evenings to watch a breathtaking sunset.

Take A Selfie With The Woolly Mammoth Statue.

"Woolly" is an ambassador of the Ice Age Trail. Sturgeon Bay is home to the Eastern Terminus of the 1200 mile trail and is just one of its Trail Communities. It's a fabulous way to call attention to this Wisconsin treasure.

10 West Larch Street in Bayview Park

The Miller Art Museum

Door County's only fine art museum is inside the Door County Library. This museum showcases a diverse range of art, including 20th Century works by Wisconsin artists. It has an entire wing dedicated to Door County artist Gerhard CF Miller. It's a delightful discovery for art enthusiasts.

107 South 4th Avenue

millerartmuseum.org

Door County Historical Museum

The Chicago Tribune named this museum one of the "Best Small Museums in the Midwest." This museum is a treasure trove of local history. It features exhibits on the area's natural history, early settlers, and industries. The museum is well-known for its dioramas of historical scenes, a wildlife exhibit with native animals, and the seasonal 'Seasons of Life' exhibit that portrays life in Door County throughout the years. It's an essential visit for those interested in the rich history and heritage of Sturgeon Bay and Door County.

18 North 4th Avenue

doorcountymuseum.org

Shopping

Cornucopia Kitchen Shop

The colorful facade of this store begs for you to enter. A haven for cooking enthusiasts, Cornucopia offers a wide range of kitchen gadgets, cookware, and gourmet foods. It's the ideal place to find that special kitchen tool you've been looking for or to discover new culinary delights. This is my favorite shop in Sturgeon Bay.

139 North 3rd Avenue

cornucopiadoorcounty.com

Dancing Bear Toys

A magical toy shop that delights children and adults alike. Dancing Bear Toys offers an array of unique, high-quality toys, games, and books, promoting imaginative and educational play. It's a must-visit for families and anyone young at heart.

13 North 3rd Avenue

Phone: (920) 746-5223

Lola May's Boutique

This trendy boutique offers a great selection of women's clothing, jewelry, and accessories. With a focus on fashion-forward and comfortable styles, it's the perfect place to find a new outfit that combines comfort with chic. This shop, along with several others, is inside The Marketplace.

58 North 3rd Avenue

lolamays.com

On Deck Clothing Company

A stylish clothing store offering a range of men's and women's fashion, accessories, and footwear. Known for its quality brands and coastal casual style. On the lower level, you will find the outlet store.

265 North 3rd Avenue

ondeckclothing.com/sturgeon-bay

Monticello On Jefferson

This charming boutique has gained a reputation for its beautiful selection of home décor, gifts, and accessories. It's a great spot for finding unique, stylish items to adorn your home or as thoughtful gifts for loved ones. The store's cozy and welcoming atmosphere makes shopping a real pleasure.

715 Jefferson Street

Phone: (920) 746-4100

FairyTail Couture Boutique

This shop has a unique selection of high-end children's clothing and toys.

41 North 3rd Avenue

Phone: (920) 851-5503

OtherWorlds Books And More

A haven for book lovers, this store offers a wide selection of books, including rare and out-of-print titles. It's a cozy spot to find your next favorite read. It's also a place for dedicated gamers and has two rooms for structured gaming.

41 North 3rd Avenue

otherworldssturgeonbay.com

Renard's Cheese

While primarily a cheese shop known for its wide selection of artisan and local cheeses, Renard's also offers a variety of other local products, making it the best place in Door County to experience Wisconsin's famous dairy delights.

2189 County Road DK

renardscheese.com

Places To Eat And Drink In Sturgeon Bay

Coffee and Bakery

5&J Coffee House

This coffee shop just oozes charm and judging by all the accolades it has received, I can see why it's so popular. Known for its cozy atmosphere and delicious coffee, this local favorite is wonderful for a relaxing break. They offer a variety of espresso drinks, teas, and light bites in a welcoming environment. Grab a delicious breakfast or lunch.

232 North 5th Avenue

5thandjefferson.com

Scaturo's Baking Co & Cafe

This bakery and café is a local favorite, known for its homemade pastries, bread, and a full breakfast and lunch menu along with pizza and Friday Fish Fry. The cozy atmosphere and delicious offerings make it a must-visit for a comforting meal.

19 Green Bay Road

scaturos.com

Kick Coffee

This lively café in the heart of downtown offers a great selection of coffee, smoothies, and baked goods. I love the seasonal drink offerings. If it's in season, try the Beet Root White Chocolate Mocha. There are gluten-free and vegan breakfast options too. The inviting atmosphere makes it a perfect spot for meeting friends or enjoying a quiet moment alone.

148 North 3rd Avenue

kickcoffeeshop.com

Restaurants

Nightingale Supper Club

A classic Wisconsin supper club, Nightingale offers a warm, retro atmosphere and is popular for its prime rib, seafood, and traditional supper club fare. It's really a Sturgeon Bay institution, opening first as a cafe in 1913. It's a great place for a hearty meal and a taste of local history.

1541 Egg Harbor Road

nightingalesupperclub.com

Door County Fire Company

Set in a historic fire station, this restaurant offers a unique dining experience with its eclectic décor and welcoming ambiance. The menu features a variety of American cuisine, including juicy burgers, steaks, and a selection of local beers.

38 South 3rd Avenue

doorcountyfirecompany.com

Kitty O'Reilleys Irish Pub

This lively Irish pub not only offers great food but also a wide selection of beers and cocktails in a festive atmosphere. Serving up traditional Irish favorites such as Beef Boxty and Irish Stew, and also plenty of other favorites like burgers and grilled salmon. Kitty's is a popular spot for both locals and visitors.

59 East Oak Street

kittyoreillys.com

Sonny's

Everyone flocks to Sonny's for its Italian dishes. The pizza is popular and so is the pasta. I love the Chicken Alfredo. Be prepared because the servings are ginormous and I can guarantee you will leave with a doggie bag. Sonny's is lively and the waterfront location makes it even more of a draw.

129 North Madison Avenue

sonnyspizzeria.com

The Bluefront Cafe

Known for its locally sourced ingredients and creative menu, Bluefront Cafe offers a modern twist on American classics. The relaxed and welcoming atmosphere makes it a favorite for both lunch and dinner. This is the spot for lighter options along with vegetarian and vegan options.

86 West Maple Street

thebluefrontcafe.com

Greystone Castle

Care for an elk sandwich? How about venison? Not only does Greystone Castle serve wild game, they have a room full of wildlife mounts. If game isn't your thing, this family friendly restaurant and bar serves burgers, steaks, and Friday Fish Fry.

8 North Madison Avenue

greystonecastlebar.com

Trattoria Del Santo

This charming Italian restaurant offers an intimate dining experience. Known for authentic Italian dishes and excellent wine selection, it's an ideal location for a romantic dinner.

117 North 3rd Avenue

trattoriadalsanto.com

Bars, Wineries, and Breweries

Bridge Up Brewing

Just down the stairs from Sonny's is Bridge Up Brewing. Spin some records and enjoy the welcoming atmosphere and diverse selection of craft beers. From hoppy IPAs to rich stouts and everything in between, there's a brew for every taste. The brewery often features live music and events, making it a lively spot for enjoying a night out. Definitely my favorite stop in town.

129 North Madison Avenue

bridgeupbrewing.com

Starboard Brewing

A microbrewery known for its artisanal craft beers. The cozy taproom offers a rotating selection of beers, brewed on-site, catering to all tastes from IPAs to smooth stouts. Come play board games while sipping a pale ale.

151 North 3rd Avenue

starboardbrewing.com

Waterfront Mary's Bar & Grill

I could have listed Waterfront Mary's under restaurants, but put it under this section because of the fun waterfront atmosphere. Sure there's a selection of food available, but the major draw in my book is the spectacular view while enjoying drinks and live music.

3662 North Duluth Avenue

waterfrontmarysbarandgrill.com

Sweet Treats

Door County Candy

This classic candy store is a paradise for those who love sweets. From homemade fudge, ice cream, and chocolates to a vast selection of candies, there's something to delight every taste. It's a great place to find a special treat or a gift to take home. I can never resist a candy store!

12 North 3rd Avenue

doorcountycandy.com

Accommodations

Hotels and Bed and Breakfast

Holiday Music Motel

This is hands down the most unique motel listed in this guide. This eclectic and fun motel is music-themed, offering a unique stay experience. It's known for its retro vibe and friendly atmosphere, not to mention the occasional live music session. Collaborative song-writing retreats are hosted at Holiday Music Motel, and you can listen to the results on Steel Bridge Radio through the app or online. It's an excellent option for music lovers and those in search of a low-key experience.

30 North 1st Avenue

White Lace Inn

This romantic Victorian bed and breakfast is known for its 18 beautifully decorated rooms, each with its own unique charm. Nestled among gardens and winding paths, it's the perfect retreat for couples looking for a peaceful and intimate stay.

16 North 5th Avenue

whitelaceinn.com

Stone Harbor Resort

Offering luxurious accommodations with stunning views of the water, Stone Harbor Resort features a range of amenities, including a restaurant, bar, and indoor pool. It's best for visitors looking for a full-service hotel in the heart of Sturgeon Bay. (Photo page 180)

107 North 1st Avenue

stoneharbor-resort.com

The Lodge At Leathem Smith

Known for its cozy and welcoming atmosphere, this lodge offers comfortable accommodations with a touch of local history. It's a great place for those looking to explore Sturgeon Bay and the surrounding area. There are accommodations from suites to double queen rooms steps away from the waterfront. If that doesn't convince you to stay here, maybe the Tiki Bar will.

1640 Memorial Drive

thelodgeatls.com

Westwood Shores

This waterfront resort offers scenic views of the bay, along with spacious suites equipped with kitchens and balconies. It's ideal for families or couples looking for a self-sufficient stay in a beautiful location.

4303 Bay Shore Drive

westwoodshores.net

The Foxglove Inn

A luxurious bed and breakfast that offers elegantly appointed rooms with attention to detail. The inn provides a perfect blend of historic charm and modern comforts, making it a best choice for those seeking a pampered experience.

344 North Avenue

foxglovedoorcounty.com

Campgrounds

Potawatomi State Park

On the shores of Sturgeon Bay, this state park offers a variety of camping options, including sites with electric hookups and access to hiking trails, boating, and fishing. It's perfect for nature lovers wanting to stay close to the city while enjoying the great outdoors.

3740 Park Drive

Tranquil Timbers Camping Resort

This campground is a peaceful retreat offering a range of camping options from tent sites to cabin rentals. With amenities like a swimming pool, mini-golf, and planned activities, it's ideal for families looking for a fun and comfortable camping experience. This campground butts up to the state park, so you can access the trails from this campground.

3668 Grondin Road

thousandtrails.com/wisconsin/tranquil-timbers-camping-resort

Door County

Writing a whole chapter on Door County is a bit of a challenge. For one thing, I could write a whole book on visiting Door County. Depending on who you ask, Door County is in the top five, if not the number one tourist destination in Wisconsin. Even though I leave Sturgeon Bay, Washington Island, and Algoma out of this chapter (they have their own chapters), there is still an abundance of places and things to do.

Like all chapters in this book, this one doesn't cover everything to enjoy in Door County, but instead covers the major points, along with some surprises. (I hope).

I highly suggest stopping at the Destination Door County Visitors Center. You will find helpful staff, along with all the information you can fit in a bag about things to do and see, so many that I cannot possibly cover them all in this chapter.

Destination Door County Visitors Center

1015 Green Bay Road, Sturgeon Bay

I absolutely adore Door County. Dubbed "the thumb", it holds magical discoveries. Many Wisconsinites avoid this popular destination during peak season. It's crazy busy. Its coastal towns ooze charm, with a nod to quaint East Coast summer retreats. Flanked by the Bay of Green Bay and Lake Michigan, each side of the

Door County peninsula has its own character. The lake side is quiet. It's a perfect choice for a stay if you want to relax and catch a perfect sunrise, spending your vacation in quiet solitude, reading and recharging. In contrast, the bay side is lively, busy with families wandering in and out of shops, spending time hiking and biking in Peninsula State Park, enjoying all the water sports, catching the perfect sunset, and enjoying a fabulous meal at one of the MANY restaurants. For variety, I like to stay on the lake side and drive over to the bay side, when I want a little action.

Location

To get to Door County from the south you can take the scenic route and follow highway 42 along the lakeshore from Algoma. Or you can jump on I-43 and once you get to Green Bay, the interstate splits off at University Avenue and takes you north to Door County.

Door County Facts

- Door County comprises small communities that line both shorelines. Sturgeon Bay is the largest city, followed by Carlsville, Egg Harbor, Fish Creek, Ephraim, Sister Bay, Ellison Bay, and Gills Rock at the tip of the peninsula. Going down the lakeside are Rowleys Bay, Baileys Harbor, and Jacksonport.

- French explorers named Door County after the treacherous water passage between the peninsula and Washington Island. They named it "Porte des Morts" which translates to "Death's Door".

- In the late 1800s and early 1900s, Scandinavians, particularly people from Iceland and Norway, immigrated to Door County in large numbers, significantly influencing its culture and cuisine.

- Door County was a focal point during Prohibition; its long coastline and numerous harbors and inlets were ideal for rum-runners bringing in alcohol from Canada.

- During the 1930s, Door County started to gain a reputation as an artist's retreat, leading to the establishment of the Peninsula School of Art and the Fish Creek Art Colony.

How Much Time To Spend In Door County

Door County has enough to do that visitors can spend a week exploring. It is one of the major tourist destinations in Wisconsin. You will also find an abundance of weekend warriors enjoying the county, as well as seasonal residents.

Things To Do In Door County

Door County Highlights

Lighthouses

Cana Island Lighthouse- One of Door County's most iconic lighthouses, Cana Island Lighthouse offers breathtaking views from its tower. The lighthouse dates back to 1869 and is accessible via a short walk across a causeway. The lighthouse is open seasonally and there is an admission to the grounds.

8800 E Cana Island Road, Baileys Harbor

dcmm.org/cana-island-lighthouse

Eagle Bluff Lighthouse- This historic lighthouse inside Peninsula State Park, built in 1868, offers a glimpse into the life of a 19th-century lighthouse keeper. The lighthouse is well-maintained, and guided tours provide insights into its history and operation. There are tours inside available seasonally. State Park admission sticker required.

Shore Road, Fish Creek

dnr.wisconsin.gov/topic/parks/peninsula/lighthouse

Baileys Harbor Range Lights-These unique range lights, built in 1869, are within The Ridges Sanctuary. While the buildings themselves are not open for tours, visitors can explore the grounds and enjoy the sanctuary's natural beauty. You cannot go inside the buildings.

8166 Highway 57, Baileys Harbor

ridgessanctuary.org/visit-us/range-lights

Old Baileys Harbor Birdcage Lighthouse- This unique and historic lighthouse, known for its "birdcage" lantern room, is one of the few remaining of its kind in the United States. It was only used from 1853 through 1869, since it was replaced by Cana Island Lighthouse. Although the remaining lighthouse and grounds are not open to the public, visitors can view it from the water.

Cave Point County Park

You cannot miss visiting Cave Point County Park, known for its breathtaking underwater caves and limestone cliffs carved by the waves of Lake Michigan. The thunderous sound of waves crashing and the panoramic views of the lake make it a year-round favorite spot for photographers and nature enthusiasts. In winter, the site treats visitors to a spectacular view. Just be sure to watch your footing. The rocks are often covered in ice. In warmer months, take a kayak tour along its 900 feet of coastline, which provides a unique perspective of the geological formations. The 18.6 acre park offers a fun half-mile trail, a picnic area, restrooms, and a small gazebo.

5360 Schauer Rd, Sturgeon Bay, WI 54235

co.door.wi.gov/554/Cave-Point-County-Park

Peninsula State Park

Spanning more than 3,700 acres, Peninsula State Park is a haven for outdoor lovers. It features majestic bluffs, serene forests, and picturesque views of Green Bay. The newest draw is the Eagle Tower, an accessible viewing tower with views of the Bay of Green Bay. Peninsula State Park is perfect for hiking, biking, and camping. The Sunset Bike Route and Eagle Trail are popular among visitors. The park's outdoor theater, Northern Sky Theater, offers performances in a unique woodland setting. If you're a golfer, the park has you covered with an 18-hole golf course. If that's not enough, you will find Eagle Bluff Lighthouse in the park. You can easily spend the whole day in the park. Wisconsin State Park admission sticker or day pass required.

9462 Shore Road, Fish Creek

dnr.wisconsin.gov/topic/parks/peninsula

The Ridges Sanctuary

As Wisconsin's oldest private nature preserve, The Ridges Sanctuary encompasses diverse habitats, including ridges and swales formed by the changing Lake Michigan shoreline. It's known for rare orchids and the Baileys Harbor Range Lights. The sanctuary offers guided nature walks, educational programs, and is a haven for birdwatchers.

8166 Hwy 57, Baileys Harbor

ridgessanctuary.org

Newport State Park

Renowned as Wisconsin's only designated wilderness park, Newport State Park offers a serene and unspoiled natural environment. Ideal for hiking, backpacking, and stargazing, this park is part of the International Dark Sky Park. Its 11 miles of Lake Michigan shoreline provide stunning landscapes and peaceful solitude.

475 County Rd NP, Ellison Bay

dnr.wisconsin.gov/topic/parks/newport

Take A Kayak Tour

There are several companies which offer Kayak tours in Door County. If you are a little adventurous, I would suggest doing a Cave Point kayak tour. With this tour you can get up close and, if weather permits, kayak right inside the caves that are dotted along the rocky shore. It's a spectacular perspective of the cliffs and caves that you see from above when you visit Cave Point County Park.

During a Cave Point tour, you are on the lake side of Door County. Depending on the weather, this isn't your leisurely paddle. Many times, there will be big waves. Safety is of the utmost importance.

I have done this tour with Door County Adventure Tours. This tour launches from Whitefish Dunes State Park, so you will need a state park entry sticker, or a day pass. (Photo page 180)

Door County Adventure Tours

4497 Ploor Road, Sturgeon Bay

dcadventurecenter.com

Door County Kayak Tours

6329 Highway 57, Jacksonport

doorcountykayaktours.com

Cave Point Paddle and Peddle

6329 Highway 57, Jacksonport

cavepointpp.com

Shopping

Some visitors flock to Door County just for the shopping. Each town is dotted with unique shops that sell not only the required t-shirts and souvenirs, but home decor, boutique clothing, sporting supplies, and local artists' wares. You will find art galleries scattered throughout the peninsula. The towns of Fish Creek and Sister Bay have the most concentrated shopping areas, but every town offers something for the dedicated shopper. I often take a day trip to Door County just to shop. You will want to take at least a full day to browse. Be advised that several shops in Door County close for the winter season.

Sister Golden

This mother/daughter owned shop is known for its eclectic mix of art, home goods, and jewelry, many of which are handmade and one-of-a-kind. While Sister Golden has a beautifully curated collection of rugs, jewelry, and other items, wander into co-owner Vicki's gallery in the back and you'll find her delightful prints using things curated from her garden and other items in nature. (Photo page 180)

4147 Main Street, Fish Creek

sistergolden.com

O'Meara's Irish House

A specialty shop offering a variety of Irish imports including clothing, jewelry, and gifts. This shop stocks a fine collection of Aran sweaters, and it was a delight to see they carried the very same sweater I bought in Dublin. If you're looking for a place to stay, there is a cottage available for rent.

3970 Highway 42, Fish Creek

omearasirish.com

Plum Bottom Gallery

Plum Bottom Gallery has multiple locations in Door County. The collection features over 200 national artists in the mediums of pottery, glass and metal art, wall art and jewelry. It's a family-run business which began on the Lubergers 20 acre property on Plum Bottom Road outside Egg Harbor.

4999 Plum Bottom Road, Egg Harbor

7813 Highway 42, Egg Harbor

4175 Main Street, Fish Creek

231 North 3rd. Avenue, Sturgeon Bay

plumbottomgallery.com

Robin Jay Music & Gifts

While this isn't a full service music store, it certainly has a fabulous variety of music-related gifts and other things. You will find a variety of folk instruments, music-related clothing, musical toys, and some supplies. My favorite is the wind-chime collection.

4199 Main Street, Fish Creek

robinjaymusic.com

Wood Orchard Market

Wood Orchard is always my first stop in Door County. It's always busy and there's a reason for that. Here you can get food, home decor, outside art, bakery items, and wine. It's the classic one-stop shop. We love the donuts, as well as the jams, jellies and other unique Door County items. Don't forget to grab some cherries or apples when they are in season.

8112 Highway 42, Egg Harbor

woodorchardmarket.com

Koepsel's Farm Market

For a classic old-fashioned roadside farm market, travel to the Lake Michigan side of Door County and stop at Koepsel's. I love stocking up on the jams, jellies, canned goods, and pickles to bring home. You'll also find in-season produce, cheeses, and popcorn. If you visit in fall, it's festively decorated with pumpkins, gourds, and corn stacks galore.

9669 Highway 57, Baileys Harbor

koepsels.com

Places To Eat and Drink in Door County

The Door County Fish Boil is hands down the most popular dining experience in Door County. There are several restaurants that each offer their own version of this traditional dining experience that is also a spectacle. Fish boils are a demonstration of the actual Scandinavian cooking method brought over from the early settlers of the area. I will list the most popular places to experience the fish boil under the Restaurant section

Coffee and Bakery

Buttercups Coffee

Located in Egg Harbor, this quaint coffee shop is nestled inside the Main Street Shops. It is known for its excellent coffee, breakfast items, and scones. The ambiance is inviting, making it a perfect spot for a relaxing coffee break.

7828 Highway 42, Egg Harbor

https://www.buttercupscoffee.com/

Blue Horse Cafe

Blue Horse Cafe is a favorite among locals and tourists alike. It is renowned for its exceptional coffee, including the popular "Chuck" caramel latte. The café also offers a selection of bakery, breakfast, and lunch items and has both indoor and outdoor seating options.

4113 Main Street, Fish Creek

bluehorsecafe.com

Fika Bakery & Coffeehouse

This Swedish American Bakery, located in the heart of Door County, offers a unique experience with its blend of Swedish and American baked goods. The bakery is known for its cozy atmosphere and delicious offerings. I'll have a Caramel Pecan Sticky Bun please!

3903 Highway 42, Fish Creek

fikafishcreek.com

Big Easy

A Southern-inspired establishment which focuses on bagels, beignets, and breakfast fare, including New Orleans-style treats and house-baked bagels. Who doesn't love the look of powdered sugar all over their face after eating a beignet?

7755 Highway 42, Egg Harbor

bigeasydoorcounty.com

Restaurants

Pelletier's Restaurant and Fish Boil

I mentioned the Door County Fish Boil. In my opinion it's a must-do experience in Door County. Pelletier's Restaurant offers nightly fish boils called "Boil Overs" with two nightly seatings, starting at 5:00 p.m. Call for reservations. Pelletier's recommends arriving 45 to 60 minutes early to enjoy the full experience.

4199 Main Street, Fish Creek

doorcountyfishboil.com

White Gull Inn

This restaurant in Fish Creek provides a quintessential Door County fish boil experience in a beautiful setting. They have seatings from May to October on Wednesday, Friday, Saturday, and Sunday evenings, and in winter, seatings on Fridays.

The Inn also invites guests to stay overnight, either in one of the rooms or a cottage, and serves breakfast, lunch, and a candlelit dinner.

4225 Main Street, Fish Creek

whitegullinn.com

Old Post Office Restaurant

Let me just say, If you want a breathtaking sunset view over the water while you enjoy your fish boil, choose the Old Post Office. The historical building was built in 1874 and was the site of a general store. The original post office was at the back of the store. The current chef's ancestors were some of the first settlers in Door County. Its fish boils are nightly and reservations can be made by calling ahead. The Old Post Office also serves breakfast.

10040 Water Street, Highway 42, Ephraim

oldpostoffice-doorcounty.com

Wild Tomato

Specializing in mouthwatering pizza, this restaurant sources its ingredients from local farms. With locations in Fish Creek and Sister Bay, it's a go-to for pizza lovers. I highly recommend getting the cheese curds here. They are some of the best I've eaten. As far as pizza goes, Packer fans will love The Green and Gold pizza.

4023 Highway 42, Fish Creek

10677 North Bay Shore Road, Sister Bay

wildtomatopizza.com

Thyme Restaurant

This restaurant can be found off the beaten path in Sister Bay. It has an upscale tasty menu featuring small bits, pizza, sandwiches, and entrees. They also have specialty menu nights. Try the Crispy Chicken Cherry Bomb. Literally a flavor explosion in your mouth,

10339 Highway 57, Sister Bay

thymedoorcounty.com

Hugel Haus

Otherwise known as "Door County's Wurst Bar", this is authentic German eating in Door County. Classic menu items such as Wienerschnitzel sit alongside Seared Salmon. If you're not a fan of the traditional schnitzel, try it done with portabella mushroom for a vegetarian twist. Don't forget to try the cheese curds or a pretzel.

11934 Highway 42, Ellison Bay

hugelhausdoorcounty.com

Al Johnson's Swedish Restaurant

This unique iconic spot in Sister Bay serves traditional Swedish cuisine like Swedish pancakes and meatballs. It's also famous for the live goats grazing on its grass-covered roof. Al Johnson's also has a nice gift shop where you can purchase many Swedish items, including Swedish pancake mix. It's a fun stop for the whole family. If you can't stop in, you can see the goats on the Goat Cam on the restaurant's website. In season, of course.

10698 North Bay Shore Drive, Sister Bay

aljohnsons.com

Bars, Wine, and Breweries

One Barrel Brewing

My favorite brewery in Door County is One Barrel. They have a huge variety of small batch brews from IPA's, ciders, hard seltzers, lagers, and specialty batches. The bonus is Pizza Bros is inside the taproom, and its pizzas are sensational. Pizza and a beer! Classic.

4633 Market Street, Egg Harbor

onebarrelbrewing.com

Peach Barn Farmhouse and Brewery

There's no finer setting to enjoy a local brew that Peach Barn. The park-like property is spacious, with many seating areas. There's over 15 different brews and seltzers made in house. This is a great spot to enjoy live music with friends, or on your own.

2450 South Bay Shore Drive, Sister Bay

peachbarnbrewing.com

Island Orchard Cider

To take advantage of the fruits of Door County, Island Orchard Cider is inviting you to come in, get a flight, and ponder the different tastes. The fruit comes from an orchard on Washington Island. I grab my flight on a sunny day and head to a table outside. (Photo page 180)

120040 Garrett Bay Road, Ellison Bay

islandorchardcider.com

Wineries

Door County is dotted with many wineries. I have some favorites that I will list. To get an overall sampling of these wineries, I would suggest going on a wine tour. Door County Trolley Inc. has a few different wine tours to choose from.

Door County Trolley Inc.

8030 Highway 42, Egg Harbor

doorcountytrolley.com

Here are some of my favorite stops for wine in Door County. All have tastings either for a fee or free.

Door 44 Vineyard and Winery

5464 County Road P, Sturgeon Bay

44wineries.com/door-44-sturgeon-bay

Door Peninsula Winery

5806 Highway 42, Carlsbad

dcwine.com

Harbor Ridge Winery

4690 Rainbow Ridge Court, Egg Harbor

harborridgewinery.com

Lautenbach's Orchard Country Winery & Market

9197 Highway 42, Fish Creek

orchardcountry.com

Sweet Treats

Ice cream shops are even more popular in Door County than wineries. I will list my favorites.

Wilson's Restaurant & Ice Cream Parlor

Sure Wilson's is a restaurant, but ice cream is the big draw. The waterfront view, red and white decor, and its location in the charming village of Ephraim makes this place even more fun. Another one of Door County's iconic establishments.

9990 Water Street, Ephraim

wilsonsicecream.com

The Candy Bar

If you find yourself on the lake side of Door County, stop at The Candy Bar in Baileys Harbor.

8113 Highway 57, Baileys Harbor

Phone: 920-609-4833

Sara's Artisan Gelato

A seasonal gelato shop that serves small batch artisan gelato and other yummy treats.

4192 Main Street, Fish Creek

sarasartisangelato.com

Door County Ice Cream Factory & Sandwich Shoppe

All the ice cream served is made here. Owner Todd Frisoni was just 21 when he purchased the shop in 2000, keeping the tradition alive. The business also serves sandwiches and pizza.

11051 Highway 42, Sister Bay

doorcountyicecream.com

Accommodations

Hotels and Bed and Breakfast

Blacksmith Inn On The Shore

This 15 room B&B stands out for its stunning location and exceptional service, ideal for those looking for a memorable stay. This is an adults-only property in Baileys Harbor. Each room has its own private bath, fireplace, and balcony.

8152 Highway 57, Baileys Harbor

theblacksmithinn.com

White Gull Inn

You won't have to go far for your fish boil if you enjoy a stay here. The main house has rooms, and there are also various sizes of cottages to rent.

4225 Main Street, Fish Creek

whitegullinn.com

Country House Resort

This is a larger resort with 46 rooms available. It is adults only, 13 and above, in a serene setting on 27 acres. It has plenty of water frontage for enjoying the sunset. If you want a place to stay with lots of amenities, choose Country House.

2486 Sunnyside Road, Sister Bay

countryhouseresort.com

Applecreek Resort

Accommodations include whirlpool tubs, fireplace, and mini-kitchen in the suites. Within walking distance to Peninsula State Park and nearby shopping.

Highway 42 and County Road F. Fish Creek

applecreekresort.com

Downtown Inn

This budget friendly motel and cottages are right in the heart of Sister Bay. You're able to walk to shopping, the marina, and the beach. The rooms are clean and comfortable.

10628 North Bay Shore Drive, Sister Bay

downtowninnsisterbay.com

Campgrounds

Peninsula State Park

Peninsula State Park has four separate sections for camping. One would think with 468 campsites and four group camping areas, it would be easy to secure a spot. No such luck, as with most Wisconsin State Parks that book 11 months in advance, it's hard to secure a spot at the last minute. You can get notified through the reservation system when cancellations occur for your selected dates.

Fish Creek

dnr.wisconsin.gov/topic/parks/peninsula/recreation/camping

Wagon Trail Campground

Wagon Trail is a campers favorite in Door County. Its location near the tip of the peninsula makes for a quiet stay. The downside, of course, is you'll need to drive everywhere. I love this campground. Full hookups are available.

1190 County Road ZZ, Ellison Bay

wagontrailcampground.com

Rustic Timbers Door County Camping LLC.

There are 100 campsites, five rustic cabins, and 15 deluxe cabins available on 80 acres. This is a full-service campground with many amenities. Pool, pub, camp store, playground and laundry facilities.

4906 Court Road, Egg Harbor

rustictimbersdoorcountycamping.com

WASHINGTON ISLAND

IMAGINE A PLACE WHERE the rush of the modern world fades into the serene rhythms of nature and history–that's Washington Island. This enchanting harbor town, set like a jewel at the northern tip of Wisconsin's Door Peninsula, is more than just a destination; it's a portal to an older, more magical world. The island is only accessible by a scenic ferry ride across a water passage known as Death's Door. It promises unspoiled beauty, a vibrant cultural heritage, and a serene ambiance.

As you step off the ferry, the charm of Washington Island unfolds before you. The air is fresher here, filled with the gentle scent of wildflowers and the invigorating tang of lake breezes. The landscape is filled with forests, shorelines, fields, farmsteads, and cottages. Washington Island's slow pace encourages you to let go of daily worries and enjoy simpler pleasures. Welcome to island time.

Here, the deep roots of Scandinavian heritage are proudly displayed in architecture and the warm hospitality of the islanders. The island is brimming with stories, from its historic settlement to the beautiful limestone pebbles at Schoolhouse Beach. While exploring the island, you'll be enchanted by charming local shops, beautiful lavender fields, and the calming sound of Lake Michigan waves.

Washington Island isn't just a place to visit; it's a world to be discovered. So grab a lavender ice cream and a shot of Bitters (a local tradition) and let's find out more.

Location

Washington Island is about seven miles northeast of the tip of the Door Peninsula in Door County. It is accessible via the Washington Island Ferry Line (car and passenger), which departs from Northport Pier at the end of Highway 42. Or for passengers only, you can depart at Gill's Rock on the Island Clipper. Crossing Death's Door, the strait between Green Bay and Lake Michigan, is a charming and unforgettable experience of Washington Island.

Washington Island Facts

- Washington Island's name is a tribute to George Washington. It reflects the deep respect and admiration for the first President of the United States, a figure symbolizing integrity and leadership.

- The island's Scandinavian heritage is a vibrant thread in its cultural fabric. This legacy is celebrated in the community's traditions, architecture, and annual festivals, which imbue the island with a distinctive Nordic charm.

- Established by Icelandic immigrants, Washington Island proudly holds the title of the oldest Icelandic settlement in the United States. This rich history is clear in the island's culture, food, and community events, offering a unique glimpse into Icelandic traditions.

- The island's location at the gateway of Death's Door, a notorious strait, has given it a significant maritime history. Shipwrecks and tales of nautical lore are woven into the island's identity, reflecting a legacy of resilience and navigation.

- With a population of 708 (2010), the island community is tight-knit, yet welcoming to visitors. This small population swells during the summer months as visitors arrive, drawn by the island's charm and serenity.

How Much Time To Spend On Washington Island

A single day on the island can provide a glimpse into its charm, allowing you to visit key sites like Schoolhouse Beach, the lavender fields, and the Jacobsen Museum. If time permits, extending your stay to a full weekend or even longer allows for a more immersive experience. You can explore the island's charming shops, enjoy its natural beauty, and maybe attend a local festival. You can enjoy biking, hiking, and wildlife-watching during your visit to Washington Island.

Getting Around Washington Island

If you take the Washington Island Ferry, you can bring your car, motorcycle, or bike on that ferry. If you'd rather not, there are options for transportation on the island. Both of the ferry lines offer tour trams that will take you to key stops on the island. You can also rent a bike, moped, or UTV to get around. Of course, these last options offer more flexibility. Here are some rental companies. Some offer other types of rentals, such as kayaks, paddle boards, and boats.

Island Adventure Company

164 Green Bay Road

islandadventurecompany.com

For all your rental needs. UTV, ebikes, kayak, paddle boards.

Annie's Island Moped Rentals

288 Lobdell Point Road

islandadventurecompany.com

Single rider mopeds.

Dor Cros Inn Island Rides Bicycle Rentals

1922 Lobdell Point Road

dorcrosinn.com/Island-Rides

Various types of bike rentals.

Things To Do In Washington Island

Washington Island Highlights

Lighthouses

These three lighthouses are not on Washington Island, but are worth mentioning since they are close. Pottawatomie Lighthouse is the only one that is open to the public for tours at specific times. A visit to the website listed can give you up-to-date information.

Pottawatomie Lighthouse- The Pottawatomie Lighthouse, located on Rock Island, just a short ferry ride from Washington Island, is Wisconsin's oldest lighthouse. It offers a glimpse into the maritime history of the region and provides stunning views of the surrounding waters. The lighthouse has been fully restored and furnished to reflect its 19th-century appearance. The lighthouse is open to the public for tours during specific times, typically from late spring to early fall. Visitors can enjoy guided tours that provide historical insights about the lighthouse and its keepers. The surrounding area is excellent for hiking and exploring Rock Island's natural beauty.

Rock Island State Park, accessible by ferry from Washington Island

dnr.wisconsin.gov/topic/parks/rockisland/lighthouse

Pilot Island Lighthouse- While not directly accessible to the public, the Pilot Island Lighthouse is a historic beacon that can be viewed from boat tours around the area. It stands as a testament to the challenging navigation of Death's Door passage. The lighthouse is an iconic structure, rich in maritime lore. Boat tours in the vicinity offer excellent opportunities to view and photograph the lighthouse.

Viewable from boat tours around Death's Door and Washington Island

Plum Island Range Lights- The Plum Island Range Lights consist of a pair of lighthouses that historically helped guide ships through the Porte des Morts (Death's Door) Strait. The front and rear range lights are distinctive in their design and are part of a larger complex, which includes a keeper's house and other structures. The range lights are occasionally open for public tours during special events. Restoration efforts are ongoing to preserve these historical structures.

Visitors can learn about the history of the range lights and maritime navigation in the area. The island is also a habitat for diverse bird species, making it a point of interest for bird watching.

Plum Island, viewable by boat

Schoolhouse Beach Park

Schoolhouse Beach is renowned for its unique smooth limestone pebbles and clear waters, it is not only a geological wonder but also an ideal spot for swimming and sunbathing. The beach's pebbles, shaped by millennia of wave action, are a rare sight, making it one of the few such beaches in the world. Enjoy swimming in the crystal-clear waters, picnicking along the shore, or simply relaxing and soaking up the sun. Kayaking and paddle boarding are also popular here, providing a unique way to explore the shoreline.

Schoolhouse Beach Road, Washington Island

washingtonisland.com/school-house-beach

Jacobsen Museum

This museum, nestled in a historic log cabin, offers a treasure trove of local natural history, Native American artifacts, and island lore. It's a compact but rich educational experience.

Natural beauty surrounds the museum, ideal for leisurely walks or nature photography. Nearby trails offer peaceful hiking opportunities.

2150 Little Lake Road

.doorcounty.com/business-directory/recreation/jacobsen-museum

Lavender Fields of Fragrant Isle

As the largest lavender farm in the Midwest, Fragrant Isle offers a sensory explosion with its vibrant lavender fields. Visitors can tour the fields, learn about lavender cultivation, and visit the on-site shop. Walking through the lavender fields is not only picturesque but also therapeutic. The farm often hosts yoga sessions amidst the lavender, providing a uniquely calming experience.

1350 Airport Road

fragrantisle.com

Stavkirke

The Stavkirke on Washington Island is a must-see architectural marvel. This church is a replica of medieval Norwegian Stave churches, characterized by their unique timber framing and intricate wood carvings. The Stavkirke on Washington Island blends historical Scandinavian design with spiritual significance, creating a serene and contemplative atmosphere. Its construction is a testament to the island's Scandinavian heritage and the craftsmanship skills of the local community. Surrounded by a peaceful forest, the Stavkirke is not just a place for quiet reflection, but also a starting point for exploring the adjacent wooded trails. The trails around the church are perfect for a peaceful walk, allowing visitors to enjoy the tranquility of the island's natural setting.

1763 Town Line Road

washingtonisland.com/stavkirke

Percy Johnson County Park

Percy Johnson County Park offers a serene beach experience with its sandy shores and clear waters. It's an ideal spot for swimming, sunbathing, and picnicking. The park also has playground and picnic areas, making it perfect for families. Besides beach activities, the park is magnificent for beach combing, bird watching, and enjoying stunning sunsets.

868 South Hemlock Drive

co.door.wi.gov/543/Percy-Johnson-County-Park

Rock Island State Park

Just a short boat ride from Washington Island, Rock Island State Park is a pristine natural area offering rugged beauty and historical sites, including the Pottawatomie Lighthouse. The park is car-free, enhancing its peaceful atmosphere.

Outdoor Activities: Hiking, camping, swimming, and exploring the lighthouse are popular activities here. The park's trails provide breathtaking views of the surrounding waters and landscapes.

Rock Island

dnr.wisconsin.gov/topic/parks/rockisland

Little Lake Nature Preserve

This tranquil nature preserve surrounds Little Lake, a small, inland lake with diverse ecosystems. It's a peaceful retreat for nature lovers, offering a quiet spot away from the more visited areas. Walking trails around the lake are perfect for nature walks and wildlife observation. Photography enthusiasts will find plenty of picturesque scenes to capture.

Little Lake Road, Washington Island

https://www.doorcountylandtrust.org

Mountain Park Lookout Tower

The Mountain Park Lookout Tower offers one of the highest vantage points on the island. Climbing the tower rewards visitors with panoramic views of the island, Green Bay, and Lake Michigan. The park surrounding the tower has trails suitable for hiking and exploring. The tower itself is a popular spot for photography.

1639 Mountain Road

doorcounty.com/business-directory/recreation/mountain-park-and-lookout-tower

Shopping

Fragrant isle Lavender Farm and Shop

When you think of the fragrant fields of those tiny blooms swaying in the breeze, you may think of a trip to Provence. France native, Martine and her husband Edgar realized that the soil, weather, and geological position of Washington Island was a close match to that French region. After experimenting with a test garden, they gave it a go and went forward with Fragrant Isle. As the largest lavender farm in the Midwest, Fragrant Isle offers an extensive selection of lavender products, including culinary lavender. The farm also has a beautiful field that visitors can tour. They also have several events during the summer season and visitors flock from all over to see the gardens in full bloom. I absolutely love the lavender ice cream and I can't leave without a lavender macaron or two.

1350 Airport Road

fragrantisle.com

Mann's Mercantile

Mann's Mercantile is a classic general store with an array of products. You'll find everything from clothing and souvenirs to hardware and groceries. Oh and they have fudge!!

1176 Main Road

shopmannsmerc.com

Sievers School of Fiber Arts

This unique shop offers a range of fiber arts supplies, including yarn, tools, and books. They also host classes and workshops for those interested in learning various fiber arts techniques. Open seasonally.

986 Jackson Harbor Road

sieversschool.com

Island Outpost

A delightful store that features a variety of goods, including brand name sportswear, home decor, and local artisan crafts. It's a great place to find a unique souvenir or gift.

268 Lobdell Point Road

islandoutpostwi.com

Fair Isle Books and Gifts

I absolutely love this shop. Unique fair trade gifts, from metal art, kids' games and felted dolls, to journals and pens. It's a super cool place to explore. It's the place on the island to get books too.

1885 Detroit Harbor Road

fairisleshop.com

Places To Eat and Drink On Washington Island

Coffee and Bakery

The Red Cup Coffee House

Known for its cozy atmosphere and excellent coffee, The Red Cup Coffee House serves freshly brewed coffee, espresso drinks, and a variety of teas. They also offer homemade baked goods, including muffins, scones, and cookies. It's a magnificent spot to relax and enjoy the laid-back island vibe. It's a local favorite and a perfect place to start your day or take a relaxing break.

1885 Detroit Harbor

Phone: (920) 847-2121

Restaurants

K.K. Fiske Restaurant & The Granary

Known for its fresh, locally harvested fish, K.K. Fiske Restaurant is a family-run establishment that specializes in traditional Door County fish boils and other seafood dishes. Plan to call ahead for a fish boil. All the whitefish options are delicious and even better because they're freshly caught!

1177 Main Road

Phone: (920) 847-2121

The Albatross Drive-In

Perfect for a quick and satisfying meal, especially if you're craving classic American drive-in food. This classic drive-in restaurant has been a staple on the island for years. Albatross serves great burgers, ice cream, and other fast-food favorites. It's known for its vintage charm and outdoor seating. New is a tiki bar called Alby's Nest across the road. Open Memorial Day to the end of October.

777 Main Road

albatrossdrivein.com

Fiddler's Green

Come here for the food and don't forget to stay for the live music. The ultra-cool stage is fashioned from a 1950's vintage camper! That's reason enough for me to visit. That's not all. This historic building was once the Detroit Harbor Schoolhouse built in the 1920's. The menu offerings include duck, brats, salmon, and vegetarian options. A real gem that garners rave reviews.

1699 Jackson Harbor Road

washingtonislandfiddlersgreen.com

The Point Grille

The Point Grille serves some great BBQ. Menu items include brisket made with their own rub, fried chicken and a homemade pimento cheese BLT. It's southern style cooking with a northern twist. Open year round. Check the website for days and hours.

164 Green Bay Road

thepointgrille.com

Bars, Wineries, and Breweries

Nelsen's Hall Bitters Pub

Nelsen's Hall isn't just a bar; it's a piece of island history. It's a must stop. Known as the home of the Bitters Club, it holds the record for the world's largest consumer of Angostura Bitters. Visitors can join the Bitters Club by taking a shot of bitters. This historic tavern, dating back to the prohibition era, offers a range of drinks in a quaint, rustic setting. They also serve food. Its atmosphere is filled with character and nostalgia, making it a must-visit for a truly unique experience.

1201 Main Road

Phone: (920) 847-2496

Accommodations

Hotels and Bed and Breakfast

Hotel Washington and Studio

This historic hotel, established in the late 1800s, exudes old-world charm. It has been beautifully restored to offer modern comforts while retaining its historic character. Each room is uniquely decorated, providing a cozy and inviting atmosphere. The hotel also features an on-site restaurant and studio space offering yoga and is available for classes and retreats. Amidst lush gardens and serene surroundings, it becomes a perfect retreat for those seeking relaxation and a touch of elegance. The second-floor rooms share two bathrooms. There is a private cottage called The Livery that has a bathroom and kitchenette.

The restaurant serves fresh dishes with food supplied by local farmers and suppliers. Seasonal only.

354 Rangeline Road

hotelwashingtonandstudio.com

Jackson Harbor Inn

This inn is on the northeastern side of the island. Perfect if you want to take a trip out to Rock Island. It's also near the Jackson Harbor Ridges State Natural area and a mile from the Washington Island Farm Museum. Most rooms have a private bath, coffeemaker, mini-fridge, and microwave. There is also a communal kitchen, and a screened-in porch. Jackson Harbor Inn is a pet-friendly property.

1899 Jackson Harbor Road

jacksonharborinn.com

Four Elements Lodging

Four Elements Lodging offers 5 adults-only cottages. The cottages are all Scandinavian style, perfect for a relaxing stay. They all have gas fireplaces and many deluxe amenities. Each cottage is for two guests with no pets allowed. The grounds are in pristine condition with a communal fire pit and courtyard. There are no TV's in the cottages, so be sure and bring a favorite book or two. Staying here is the definition of being on island time.

1934 Lobdell Point Road

fourelementslodging.com

Sunset Resort

Who would love to witness an amazing sunset every night? That's what you'll get when you stay at Sunset Resort. On the western part of Washington Island, this resort has water views from all the rooms, a sand beach, and spacious grounds. The 12 no frills rooms all have private baths. The resort does not allow pets.

889 Old West Harbor Road

sunsetresortwi.com

Campgrounds

Washington Island Campground

Yes, you can bring any size camper on the ferry. This campground is full service. The grounds have a swimming pond, playground, laundry, and more. There are 102 sites, a mix of tent, water and electric, horse sites, and one group site. Cabins are available for rent. There is also an equestrian area. Rates are reasonable and there is a dump station onsite.

745 East Side Road

washingtonislandcampground.com

Green Bay

Green Bay, a city with deep historical roots and vibrant contemporary culture, offers a multifaceted experience that attracts visitors from all walks of life. One of the city's most famous attractions is the Green Bay Packers, a professional football team that not only boasts a storied history but also a unique fan-owned structure, making Lambeau Field a pilgrimage site for sports enthusiasts.

The city's shopping scene complements this sporting spirit, with options ranging from quaint local boutiques and historic markets like the Broadway District to modern malls such as Bay Park Square, providing ample opportunities for visitors to find both artisanal crafts and popular retail goods. This blend of historic charm and modern convenience makes Green Bay a retail haven with a personal touch.

Beyond sports and shopping, Green Bay offers a wealth of outdoor recreational activities that showcase its natural beauty. From the tranquil Green Bay Botanical Garden, which explodes with color and life in every season, to the expansive wildlife sanctuaries and state parks, the city is a dream for nature lovers. These green spaces provide year-round activities, from hiking and birdwatching in the summer to cross-country skiing and ice fishing in the winter.

Green Bay's cultural scene is equally enriching, featuring museums like the Neville Public Museum, performance venues like the Meyer Theater, and public art that celebrates the city's culture.

Foodies also have their share of delights to explore, with an array of dining options that span cozy cafes, bustling breweries, and fine dining establishments, serving everything from traditional American fare to exotic international dishes, all prepared with a focus on local ingredients and innovative culinary techniques.

Green Bay offers a diverse and satisfying array of attractions, making it a compelling destination for anyone looking to immerse themselves in a city where tradition and modernity coexist harmoniously.

Location

Green Bay is located on the bay of Green Bay, a sub-basin of Lake Michigan, at the mouth of the Fox River in Northeast Wisconsin. It is approximately 45 miles from Sturgeon Bay and about 40 miles from Two Rivers and can be accessed via Interstate 43 or U.S. Highway 57 if you come from Sturgeon Bay.

Green Bay Facts

- Green Bay proudly holds the title of the oldest continuous European settlement in Wisconsin. In 1634, French explorer Jean Nicolet met the local native tribes of the Ho Chunk and Menominee at Red Banks, and established a friendly relationship with them. He named this area "La Baye." La Baye later became a center of fur trading. It wasn't until 1745 that the first permanent European settlers called this area home.

- The first newspaper in Wisconsin, "The Green Bay Intelligencer," was published in Green Bay in 1833. This publication highlights Green Bay's role in the early dissemination of news and information in the state, contributing to its historical significance as a center of communication and culture.

- The Green Bay Packers owe their name to an early sponsor, the Indian Packing Company, a local meatpacking firm where Curly Lambeau worked. The company provided jerseys and use of the athletic field, hence the name "Packers." Acme Packing Company bought the company in 1922 and the Packers were briefly called "Acme Packers". This unique origin of an NFL team's name underscores the deep community ties within Green Bay.

- Green Bay's population is 106,095 (2022) making it the third largest Wisconsin city (behind Milwaukee and Madison) and the second largest of our Wisconsin Harbor Towns.

How Much Time To Spend In Green Bay

Green Bay deserves at least a full weekend of exploration, with a full week to see most things, particularly if those things are football-related, since that can easily take a weekend alone.

Things To Do In Green Bay

Green Bay Highlights

Lighthouses

Grassy Island Range Lights-The Grassy Island Range Lights are a pair of lighthouses that were originally constructed in 1872 to guide ships safely through the lower Green Bay harbor to the port of Green Bay. Positioned on Grassy Island, these range lights worked by aligning vertically to provide a navigational line for ships.

Today, they are relocated to the mainland for public viewing at the Green Bay Yacht Club, where they continue to stand as symbols of Green Bay's maritime heritage. You can tour the structures for free.

100 Bay Beach Road

greenbayyachtclub.com

Green Bay Harbor Entrance Lighthouse-The Green Bay Harbor Entrance Light, also known as the Green Bay Entrance Light, plays a critical role in navigating the waters of Green Bay, marking the main channel entrance from Lake Michigan. Established in the early 20th century, this active aid to navigation is an essential feature for the large commercial and recreational vessels that travel to and from the port facilities of Green Bay.

The light remains an active navigational aid and is not open for public tours, but it can be viewed from the shore or by boat for those interested in maritime history and navigation.

lighthousefriends.com/light.asp?ID=635

Long Tail Point Lighthouse-Another historical beacon in the area is the Long Tail Point Lighthouse, which has a history dating back to 1848. This lighthouse was essential in guiding vessels into the Green Bay port via the Long Tail Point peninsula.

The original lighthouse structure, or what remains of it, can still be seen and is part of local efforts to preserve maritime history. The Long Tail Point Lighthouse is less accessible than others but offers a glimpse into the challenging conditions faced by early lighthouse keepers and the vital role these structures played in the development of commerce in Green Bay.

Accessible by boat at Long Tail Point, Suamico

lighthousefriends.com/light.asp?ID=634

Visit Historic Lambeau Field and Titletown District

For football fans, a visit to the home of the Green Bay Packers is a pilgrimage that draws visitors from around the world. Attending a game here is an experience. I have attended several games throughout the years and this historic stadium has an energy that is second to none. Let me tell you how integral this football team is to the area. If you are in the Green Bay media market, it is Packer season all year long. Yes, we love our Green Bay Packers, and are not only proud of the fact that the team is publicly-owned, but also has a worldwide fan base.

Visiting Lambeau Field, the **Packer Pro Shop**, and the **Hall of Fame** are a necessity to understand the community significance around this team. I highly suggest taking one of the available tours. There is nothing like walking through that famed tunnel onto the field. Consider all the football greats that have preceded your footsteps. Even though I am not a huge football fan, this walk brought tears to my eyes. After your tour, enjoy lunch or dinner at **1919 Kitchen & Tap** for incredible food. Take a trolley tour on the **Packers Heritage Trail** and visit several points of interest along the way. Visitors can also walk, bike, or drive along the trail. (Photo page 241)

Just across the road from Lambeau Field is the **Titletown District**, a complex made up of restaurants, shops, a sledding hill (which is a fabulous green space in summer), ice rink, and event space. Don't leave town without loading up on Packer merchandise at the Pro Shop!

1265 Lombardi Avenue

packers.com/lambeau-field/

Heritage Hill State Historical Park

Step back in time at Heritage Hill State Historical Park. This living history museum features over 25 historic buildings from different eras of Wisconsin's past, offering interactive, educational experiences for all ages.

2640 South Webster Avenue

heritagehillgb.org

Neville Public Museum

At the Neville Public Museum, explore engaging exhibits on regional history, science, and art. This museum enriches visitors with insights into the cultural and natural history of Northeast Wisconsin and the Upper Peninsula.

210 Museum Place

nevillepublicmuseum.org

Green Bay Botanical Garden

Explore vibrant landscapes and diverse plant species at Green Bay Botanical Garden. This 47-acre sanctuary showcases gardens designed to thrive in the Upper Midwest, offering beauty and education through all four seasons. The garden is host to events and special exhibits.

2600 Larsen Road

gbbg.org

National Railroad Museum

Delve into America's rich railroad heritage at the National Railroad Museum. Featuring historic railcars, events, educational exhibits, and train rides, it's a captivating destination for history buffs and railroad fans alike. The museum is currently fundraising for an impressive expansion.

2285 South Broadway

nationalrrmuseum.org

Bay Beach Wildlife Sanctuary

The Bay Beach Wildlife Sanctuary is an urban refuge that offers a chance to connect with nature and observe local wildlife. Its educational programs and rehabilitation efforts make it a vital part of the community. There are five miles of trails within the sanctuary that can be enjoyed year-round.

1660 East Shore Drive

greenbaywi.gov/1418/Bay-Beach-Wildlife-Sanctuary

The Automobile Gallery

The Automobile Gallery is not just a museum; it's an homage to the art and history of automobiles. This "hidden gem" showcases over 100 classic and exotic cars that trace the evolution of the automobile over the past century, presented in a sophisticated space that will captivate car enthusiasts and casual visitors alike.

400 South Adams

theautomobilegalley.org

Take In A Show At the Meyer Theater

The historic Meyer Theatre is a cornerstone of Green Bay's cultural scene, offering an intimate setting for a variety of performances ranging from concerts and comedies to plays and community events. Originally opened in 1930 as one of the Fox Theatres, this restored venue retains its old-world charm while providing state-of-the-art acoustics and seating for an unforgettable entertainment experience. I recommend taking in one of the **Let Me Be Frank** productions for fun entertainment.

117 South Washington Street

meyertheater.org

Weidner Center For The Performing Arts

The Weidner Center is Green Bay's premiere venue for performing arts. Enjoy a spectrum of shows, from captivating Broadway productions to classical music performances, in this state-of-the-art facility.

2350 Weidner Center Drive

weidnercenter.org

Shopping

Broadway District

This is the main shopping district in Green Bay. You'll find over 50 shops in this area from **ZuLou** which features fashionable, comfortable clothing and home products to **Pete's Garage**, supplier of biking and skiing supplies, and **Beerntsen's Candies**.

On Wednesday nights during spring, summer, and fall, Broadway and the surrounding streets are where it's at. This is when the uber popular Broadway Farmers Market takes place. If you're in town, it's a must visit.

Broadway Street, Downtown

Lion's Mouth Bookstore

A paradise for book lovers, the Lion's Mouth Bookstore offers a wide selection of new and used books across various genres. This cozy bookstore provides a welcoming atmosphere where readers can find their next great read and participate in book signings and other community events.

211 North Washington Street

lionsmouthbookstore.com

Sunrise On Main

A beautifully curated inventory of consignment and vintage clothing and accessories for women. Part of the proceeds go to its partner mission Reset.Life, which serves women going through personal and professional transitions.

1244 Main Street, Suite 2

sunriseonmain.com

Places to eat and drink in Green Bay

Coffee and Bakery

The Attic Books & Coffee

This charming bookstore and café offers a cozy atmosphere perfect for enjoying a cup of coffee and a good book. Their selection of freshly brewed coffee and homemade bakery items makes it a favorite local hangout.

730 Bodart Street

Phone: (920) 435-6515

Kavarna Cafe

A spacious and eclectic spot, Kavarna serves as both a coffeehouse and a vegetarian café. Their extensive coffee menu is complemented by an array of baked goods, including vegan and gluten-free options. Visit for breakfast or lunch.

143 North Broadway

kavarna.com

Uncle Mike's Bake Shoppe

Renowned for winning the "Best Kringle in North America" (shhh, we won't tell Racine), Uncle Mike's Bake Shoppe is a must-visit for anyone with a sweet tooth. Their coffee and award-winning pastries make for an unbeatable combination.

2999 East Mason Street

unclemikesbakeshoppe.com

The Creamery

A cozy cafe known for its locally roasted coffees and unique breakfast and lunch menu. The Creamery offers a variety of bakery items made from scratch daily. Their comfortable seating, views from the City Deck, and friendly atmosphere provide the perfect setting for enjoying a leisurely breakfast or a coffee break.

114 Pine Street

thecreamerycafe.com

Not By Bread Alone

A cozy café and bakery known for its fresh-baked breads, delightful pastries, and hearty sandwiches. Not By Bread Alone is perfect for a quick lunch or picking up treats for a picnic.

940 Hansen Road

notbybread.com

Restaurants

Plae Bistro

Absolutely one of my favorites. Plae Bistro offers a casual yet elegant dining experience with a menu that features creative dishes made from fresh, local ingredients. The atmosphere is friendly and modern, ideal for a business lunch or a relaxing dinner. I go for lunch and seem to always order the grilled fig panini.

1671 Hoffman Road Suite 10

plaebistro.com

a'Bravo Bistro

A sophisticated spot known for its eclectic cuisine and an impressive selection of wines. A'Bravo provides a chic atmosphere perfect for a romantic dinner or a special occasion meal, but also great for a girlfriends' lunch.

2067 Central Court #77

abravobistro.com

River's Bend

Known for its classic steakhouse fare and scenic river views, River's Bend offers a traditional dining experience with a focus on quality and comfort. It's a great place for a hearty meal in a welcoming setting. This is your supper club experience in Green Bay.

792 Riverview Drive

riversbendgb.com

Kroll's West

An iconic diner famous for its butter burgers and casual dining atmosphere, Kroll's West is a Green Bay institution. It's particularly popular on game days, offering a classic Wisconsin dining experience. There's also a Kroll's East, serving burgers since 1935.

1990 South Ridge Road

krollswest.com

Al's Hamburgers

Al's Hamburger, a Green Bay staple since 1934, offers classic American diner fare at its best. Renowned for its burgers and hearty breakfasts, Al's delivers quality and nostalgia at affordable prices. I'll have a Classic ¼ hamburger and a chocolate malt please.

131 South Washington Street

alshamburgergb.com

White Dog

White Dog Cafe offers a quirky and eclectic dining experience with a menu that features creative comfort food. Known for its vibrant atmosphere and funky decor featuring local artists, this cafe is a favorite among locals who appreciate its laid-back vibe and inventive burgers and sandwiches.

201 South Broadway

whitedoggreenbay.com

While you have to head out of town to Suamico for these next two, they are worth it.

Rustique Pizza & Lounge

Set in a renovated church, Rustique provides a unique ambiance to enjoy artisan pizzas and contemporary American cuisine. It's known for its creative dishes and rustic charm. I'd say the best pizza around.

13201 Velp Avenue, Suamico

rustiquegb.com

Chives

Chives offers a unique farm-to-table dining experience, serving seasonal dishes that highlight local ingredients. The restaurant's casual yet sophisticated atmosphere makes it a popular choice for foodies.

1749 Riverside Drive, Suamico

chivesdining.com

Bars, Wineries, and Breweries

Titletown Brewing Company

A local favorite, Titletown Brewing Company offers a wide selection of craft beers brewed on-site, with a rooftop patio that provides great views of the city. You can take a brewery tour with up to 16 people. Titletown has a menu featuring daily specials.

320 North Broadway

titletownbrewing.com

Hinterland Brewery

Known for its artisanal beers and upscale pub fare, Hinterland Brewery features a modern, spacious setting right across from Lambeau Field. It's a perfect spot for a game day or a special brewery tour. You must order a small plate of brussels sprouts, if you're a fan. My favorite brew is the Chocolate Peanut Butter Meltdown.

1001 Lombardi Avenue

hinterlandbeer.com

Copper State Brewing Co.

Copper State Brewing Co. is a key player in Green Bay's craft beer scene, offering a broad range of beers brewed on-site, from IPAs to stouts. The brewery also features a café with coffee and a menu of elevated pub fare, making it a versatile spot for any time of day. I love the cozy warm atmosphere here. (Photo page 241)

313 Dousman Street

Copperstate.beer

Captain's Walk Winery

Located in a charming pre-Civil War building, Captain's Walk Winery offers a casual tasting experience without the need for a reservation. They produce small-batch wines with grapes sourced from premium vineyards across the country.

345 South Adams Street

captainswalkwinery.com

Sweet Treats

Zesty's Frozen Custard

Known for its creamy, rich frozen custard, Zesty's is the go-to spot for frozen treats in Green Bay. Their custard is made fresh daily, with a rotating menu of flavors.

508 Green Avenue

zestyscustard.com

Sara's Artisan Gelato

It's nearly impossible to resist gelato. Sara makes her own gelato using the traditional techniques and the freshest real ingredients. You can find her gelato in multiple locations too.

933 Anderson Drive

sarasartisangelato.com

Accommodations

Green Bay has a wide number of chain hotels in and around the city at different price ranges. If you are visiting during Packers home game weekends, empty rooms are hard to come by and prices are usually higher.

Hotels and Bed And Breakfast

Hotel Northland, Autograph Collection

This newly restored historic hotel combines old-world 1920s charm with modern amenities, offering a luxurious stay in the heart of Green Bay. It's perfect for those seeking a sophisticated experience. There are 160 rooms, all decorated in fresh light neutral colors with bold accents.

304 North Adams Street

marriot.com

Lodge Kohler

Located in the heart of Titletown, just steps away from Lambeau Field, Lodge Kohler offers a luxurious hospitality experience. This four-diamond hotel features sophisticated accommodations, a world-class spa, and dining options that cater to the finest tastes. Who wouldn't want a view of Lambeau Field from their hotel?

1950 South Ridge Road

lodgekohler.com

Tundra Lodge Resort and Waterpark

Offering a distinctive Northwoods theme, Tundra Lodge Resort and Waterpark provides family-friendly accommodations with an extensive indoor waterpark and conference facilities. It's ideal for families looking for fun and adventure without leaving the hotel.

865 Lombardi Avenue

tundralodge.com

The Astor House

This charming five room bed and breakfast is set in a beautifully restored Victorian house offering personalized service and a quiet, welcoming atmosphere, perfect for a relaxing getaway.

637 South Monroe

astorhouse.com

Campgrounds

Green Bay Reforestation Camp

The Green Bay Reforestation Camp offers a unique camping experience within a 1,600-acre preserve that provides a variety of outdoor activities and educational opportunities. The camp features around 50 campsites suitable for tents and RVs, some no hookups, some electric and water, and some full hookups. There's access to restrooms and showers. Campers can enjoy amenities such as hiking and mountain biking trails, wildlife viewing, a fishing pond, and the adjacent NEW Zoo and Adventure Park. Reservations can be made online.

4418 Reforestation Road

browncountywi.gov/community/parks-department/general-information/camping/#Reforestation%20Camp%20Campground

Oconto

HAVE YOU EVER DRIVEN through a town over and over throughout the years to get to a destination beyond, and were left wondering what you would find if you just made one turn onto the main street?

I've often wondered that way about Oconto, Wisconsin. Before the Highway 41 bypass was built, the highway ran right through Oconto. Growing up, we took that route often. I would dream of camping along the Oconto River at Holtwood Campground, and we would sometimes stop at Wayne's Restaurant for breakfast or lunch. Later, when my daughter Megan and I were on our way to Escanaba for summer vacation, I would often think about turning right at the only stoplight in town and exploring Oconto's Main Street. This was long before I became a travel blogger and I was just focused on getting to my destination as fast as possible.

Location

Oconto is a Wisconsin Harbor Town located off Highway 41, about 30 miles north of Green Bay. It lies on the shores of the Bay of Green Bay on Lake Michigan.

Oconto Facts

- Oconto is known as the home to the Archaic Copper Culture Indian burial ground, which is the oldest cemetery in Wisconsin and one of the oldest in the United States. This was the period between 5500 and 2500 BC. The Copper Culture settled in an area which is now known as Susie's Hill. They were known for their copper metalwork.

- By the 1860s, commercial lumbering was the principal business with 12 sawmills operating in the area. Commercial fishing was also an early industry.

- he harbor was moved to its present location in 1875 and was once a major port on the Bay of Green Bay.

- The population of Oconto is 4,575 (2021)

Oconto makes a great weekend destination, or even a great day trip. There's plenty to do. Magnificent parks, a fantastic self-guided tour of Main Street and its historic homes, shopping, and some great small businesses to discover. Oconto has a family feel, along with being the perfect spot to enjoy a laid-back, relaxed getaway.

Things To Do In Oconto

Oconto Highlights

One of my favorite things about Oconto is its fantastic network of **biking trails** throughout the city. There are six routes totaling nearly 18 miles, with the longest route being Copper Culture Trail at four miles. See the historical sites by bike or take a cruise out to the harbor. You can download a map here or pick one up at the **Oconto Visitor Center** inside the Shell station at 517 Smith Avenue.

Copper Culture State Park

Oconto is home to **Copper Culture State Park and Museum**. Copper Culture State Park marks the site of the burial grounds of the Old Copper Culture, an ancient group of natives that used the copper found around the Great Lakes to craft tools. In 1952, a 13-year-old boy discovered human bones when he was playing in what was known then as a quarry site, revealing the site of the burial grounds of the Old Copper Culture. Shortly after that, the Wisconsin Archeological Society dug up the site to learn more. The park has a monument dedicated to the burial area. You can also learn more and view photos from the dig inside the Charles Werrebroeck Museum open in summer in the park.

The park has walking trails, a picnic area, grill, and a pavilion area. There are also restrooms. There is no Wisconsin State park sticker or entry free required, but the park does take donations.

Historic Main Street

Oconto's official tagline is "History by the Bay " and there are some great things to do to explore the local history. I already mentioned Copper Culture State Park, but you can also take a self-guided walk or bike along the **Historic Main Street.** Within a three-block stretch, you can view 23 historic structures, each identified by a number along the street (numbers displayed during summer). The 21 homes you'll see are various Victorian style homes, built approximately between 1850-1905. You can find a printed map and information about each stop at the **Oconto Visitor Center** inside the Shell station at 517 Smith Avenue.

Beyer Home & Carriage Museum

After your self-guided tour, I would recommend touring the **Beyer Home & Carriage Museum**. The home was originally built in 1868 and was the county's first brick home. George and Fannie Beyer purchased the home ten years later and remodeled it in Queen Anne style. Today you can tour the home and view its Victorian furnishings and décor.

Also on the property is the George E. Hall Annex, which features an Old Main Street display and exhibits of the Old Copper culture and more.

You'll find the Carriage House Museum that includes a collection of carriages, cars, and Bond Pickle Company, a historic pickle company founded in Oconto, advertising displays.

The original barn still stands and you can also see a restored frontier log cabin.

The Beyer Home & Carriage Museum is open for from Memorial Day through Labor Day (closed on Tuesday). (Photo page 241)

917 Park Avenue

ocontohistory.org

Oconto Parks

Your first stop in Oconto should be out to Breakwater Park and Harbor. **Breakwater Park** is a small park where the Oconto River meets the bay. There is a boat landing, pavilion, and boat slips for rent. There are plenty of benches to sit on and enjoy the view. Across from the park is one of the most popular restaurants in Oconto, The Dockside.

Drive past the harbor and the restaurant and you can drive the longest causeway in North America. The views are stunning along **Splinters Causeway** as you pass by people fishing, or just admiring the view of the Bay of Green Bay. This turned out to be one of my favorite stops while visiting Oconto.

Bond Park is on Charles Street on the Oconto River. It's a great place along the city's bike and pedestrian train to stop and rest. There's a playground and exercise equipment and an amazing view of the river.

Holtwood Sporting Complex and Park and adjacent campground are right on the Oconto River. It's the perfect spot to launch your boat, kayak, paddleboard, or any other watercraft. There are pavilions, picnic areas, volleyball courts and baseball diamonds. Try your hand at disc golf at the **Mikel Wittkopf Memorial Disc Golf Course.**

Another major park in Oconto is **City Park** along the Bay of Green Bay on the south side of Oconto on Highway N. There's over 700 feet of shoreline to dip your toe in the cool water. You'll also find a picnic and playground area, pavilion, restrooms, and more. There are nine first come, first served campsites too.

Last but not least, we have the multi-use **Sharp Park** on 7th Street. Trails, tennis courts, pickleball courts, playground, and lots of open space to enjoy.

The Ruins Adventure Golf

Challenge your travel companion with a round of mini golf at The Ruins Adventure Golf. Play nine holes or go all out and play 18. This course is fun for all ages.

150 Howard Lan

theruinsgolf.com

Shopping

Oconto is more about outdoor activities than about shopping, but there are a handful of cute shops to check out. You can find some basics at a dollar store, Tractor Supply, or the local hardware store.

The Shop On Main

This place is so much more than a coffee shop, it's a place to browse through. After you sit and enjoy your coffee and cinnamon roll, or ice cream, check out all the gifts and home décor available for sale. Housed in a converted auto garage, I love the farmhouse décor with the galvanized steel on the ceilings, brick walls, its industrial rustic cool. This belongs in the places to eat category too, since it is clearly the spot to drop in for your morning coffee fix, witnessed by the number of patrons seen coming and going whenever I stop in. (Photo page 241)

821 Main Street

theshoponmainoconto.square.site

Olive and Birch

A cute boutique offering an elegant shopping experience for those who love shopping for women's and men's clothing. This shop carries fashion-forward styles at moderate prices. This store has limited hours though, so I would definitely call ahead.

1102 Main Street

Phone: (920) 604-9125

Places to eat and drink in Oconto

Coffee and Bakery

The Shop On Main

As I mentioned earlier, The Shop on Main is the place in Oconto for coffee, tea, and other specialty drinks. You can also get some baked goods here if you'd like, along with sandwiches and soups. All made on-site in the kitchen. On a hot day (or anytime you're craving ice cream), stop here.

821 Main Street

Phone: (920) 516-7062

Restaurants

River Diner and Smokehouse

If you enjoy a great BBQ, then check out River Diner and Smokehouse (formally Wayne's Family Restaurant). They have an extensive menu of smokehouse delights from loaded mac and cheese with pulled pork, to smoked chicken wings. I have had the brisket tacos and enjoyed them. Make sure you save room for pie, or order a slice to go, because this restaurant is famous for pie. River Diner and Smokehouse also serves breakfast all day.

There's plenty of seating inside.

805 Brazeau Avenue

Phone: (920) 835-4262

The Dockside

I enjoy dining at The Dockside across from Breakwater Park. In the summer, this is a busy spot, especially Friday nights when The Dockside's famous Shrimp Boil sells out fast. The menu is above average with the expected items - Friday Fish Fry, burgers, and steak - alongside the unexpected. I love the addition of such menu items as Croque Madame, Tuna Tartare, and Schnitzel. Reservations are recommended, especially during the summer months.

1302 Harbor Road

docksideoconto.com

Brothers Three

People love Brothers Three's freshly made pizza in Oconto, just like its Marinette counterpart. With a prime location on the Oconto River, you get a fabulous view when you dine in. If you don't feel like going out, they offer delivery. If pizza is not your thing, they have spaghetti, burgers, sandwiches, soups and salads.

106 Superior Avenue

/brothersthreeoconto.com

Bars, Wineries, and Breweries

The Garage

Most towns have that one bar where locals and visitors can go to feel welcomed. To relax and enjoy, mingle with the regulars, listen to live music and have a memorable time. The Garage in Oconto is that place. You know from the moment you order a brew from the extensive craft options on tap, you're at home.

The first time my friend Erin and I visited The Garage, I couldn't see the lineup of beer tappers from my spot at the bar. So, the friendly bartender invited me behind the bar to get a closer look and sample a few if I liked. Erin and I made our choice and moved to a table. Not long after, the owner, John, came over, greeted us, and made sure we had what we wanted.

That's what you'll find here. The place is small (it is a real garage), but in summer, they have a large patio space outside to relax, enjoy some bar food, and listen to live music. A 10 out of 10 for friendliness and a fun atmosphere.

1200 Main Street

Phone: (920) 834-3002

Sweet Treats

Shake-A-Burger

It's a warm summer day. You have explored Oconto on the bike trails and you crave some ice cream, or maybe a quick burger. Drive on over to Shake-A-Burger. Seating is only outside with superb views of the Oconto River, and you go inside to the window to order. If you don't feel like getting out of your car, there is a drive-thru as well.

I love the Kabooms ("a shake with attitude"), which are a take on a Dairy Queen Blizzard. There are lots of ice cream treats to choose from. Specialties like Fudge Brownie Delight, cones, malts, slushies, and more! They have a selection of burgers, hot dogs, sandwiches, and sides.

107 Brazeau Avenue

Phone: (920) 834-6200

Accommodations

Hotels

Econo Lodge Inn and Suites

Basic budget option in downtown Oconto. A member of the Choice Hotels chain. Basic rooms, indoor pool and whirlpool and pet friendly. Free Wi-Fi and breakfast.

600 Brazeau Avenue

choicehotels.com

Campgrounds

Holtwood Campground

Large 170 site campground along the Oconto River. Most sites have full hookups. Plenty of riverside grassy sites are available. Nice, clean restroom and shower building, firewood available, and small store inside the office. There are paddleboards, kayaks, canoe, river tubes, and more to rent for a few hours or the whole day at inexpensive rates.

I loved camping here because of its proximity to town and all the biking trails. The campground is connected to the sporting complex and boat landing.

400 Holtwood Way

cityofoconto.com/camping/

City Park Campground

Nine first come, first served sites. No electricity, no showers. Definitely for you if you like a quiet spot and roughing it.

County Highway N

Phone:(920) 834-7706

Marinette

Marinette is a city that I've driven through many times. My dad, an avid fisherman, trolled the Menominee River to catch his limit of walleye for as long as I can remember (still does). Many times I joined him, and after I married, my husband and I would do the same.

I never actually visited the city of Marinette other than stopping at a fast food place or a gas station right off US Highway 41 on the way to the boat landing across the river in Menominee, Michigan. I was excited to actually see this Wisconsin Harbor Town for the first time through the lens of a visitor, and to explore what makes this city tick.

Location

Marinette is located 23 miles north of Oconto. Continue on US Highway 41 and you will drive right through the middle of Marinette. Marinette, which is located 23 miles north of Oconto, is considered a "Twin City" with Menominee, Michigan, just across the bridge.

Marinette Facts

- Today's population is 11,048 (2021).

- Named after its most famous historical figure Queen Marinette, who was part Menominee Indian, part White.

- Marinette's first settlers were later known as the Menominee Indian Tribe. They settled on the banks of the Menominee River and that site is now marked with the tall bear statue you can see at Menekaunee Harbor.

- Marinette is best known for its shipbuilding industry today. Fincantieri Marinette Marine has been building ships since 1942. FMM builds ships for the US Navy, US Coast Guard, and other Governmental Agencies. If you are lucky, you will catch a ship launch on the Menominee River.

- Fishing is one of the major attractions that brings visitors to Marinette. In fact, there are seven fishing tournaments held annually in Marinette. The prime catch is walleye and on any spring, summer, or fall day, you will find anglers lined up along the shoreline on Stephenson Island and boats dotting the Menominee River.

How Much Time To Spend In Marinette

Visiting Marinette in a day will keep you quite busy. It's better to give yourself a couple of days or a long weekend to experience what Marinette offers.

Things To Do In Marinette

Marinette Highlights

Lighthouses

Unfortunately, there are no lighthouses in Marinette. You can, however, cross the bridge into Menominee, Michigan to visit the lighthouse in Ann Arbor Park.

Menominee River

The pride of Marinette is the Menominee River. The river is the center of activity in the city. Anglers come from all over to fish this famous river. There is kayaking, boating, and more recreational opportunities. The river has historical significance, as it was the settlement of the Menominee Tribe and played a major role in the logging industry.

Stephensons Island

Before you cross the bridge into Michigan on US Highway 41, to the left you will see Stephenson Island. Park your car in the large parking lot. You cannot miss the larger-than-life statue of horses pulling a lumber-filled wagon. That makes a great photo op. You'll also see the Wisconsin welcome sign up on the hill. Issac Stephenson, a prominent citizen of Marinette who made his fortune in lumber, is the namesake of Stephenson Island. He was also a US Congressman (1883-1889) and a US Senator (1907-1915).

The island, which is also a city park, is on the Menominee River. There is a playground, park pavilion, gazebo, and picnic areas. Stephenson Island is also a popular spot for anglers. On any day, you will see them lined up along the river banks with poles in the water. In honor of Marinette's logging history, you will find the Marinette County Historical Logging Museum on the island, along with the Evencheck Cabin, an example of a typical homesteaders residence. They built the cabin in 1897.

The island is a great place to spend a few quiet moments on one of the park benches, enjoying the view of the river. Don't miss the statue "The Young Swimmers" by James F. Hophensperger behind the logging museum. It became one of my favorite things in Marinette. Another statue on the island is The Soldier's

Memorial. In May 1917, they dedicated the statue as a tribute to the Marinette County soldiers who died in the Civil War.

Walk to the River Walk Bridge that crosses over the river from Stephenson Island and into Marinette. Stop in the **Wisconsin Welcome Center and Tourist Information** building. You can pick up a Historic Riverside Avenue Walking Tour brochure for your next stop.

Riverside Avenue

When you have your brochure, take a self-guided walking tour of the most historic street in Marinette. Along the street, you will find the homes of some of Marinette's most elite residents who made their mark on the history of Marinette. Most are still standing and serve as private residences, with a couple that were razed. There are various architectural styles represented such as Queen Anne, Georgian Revival, and Foursquare. You can imagine a prosperous time when these homes were the social center of the city.

Park at the **Stephenson Public Library** at 1700 Hall Avenue, cross Riverside Avenue at Hattie Court and proceed up Riverside Avenue. Give yourself an hour to read about each home and monument and to admire the facades of the remaining homes.

Among the homes on the quiet tree-lined street was the residence of Isaac Stephenson, yes, the same Isaac Stephenson that they named the island and the library after. The site where his home once stood is now a church. A statue honoring Isaac Stephenson stands on the river side of the avenue.

At 1975 Riverside Avenue, you will see the Georgian Revival home of Joseph and Cecilia Lauerman. At 23 years of age, Joseph opened a store on Main Street in Marinette and was eventually joined in this venture by his two brothers, Frank and Charles. The Lauerman Brothers Department Store would have 13 department stores in Wisconsin, Michigan, and Iowa. The flagship store in Downtown Marinette closed its doors in 1987, but the building still stands today.

Queen Marinette

A tribute to Marinette's most famous woman sits along the river on Riverside Avenue. Marie Antoinette Chevalier was born in 1793. Her father was a French trapper by the name of Bartholemy Chevalier, and her mother was the daughter of Menominee Indian Chief Wauba-Shish. She became the wife of John Jacobs when she was very young.

Jacobs and William Farnsworth went into partnership and took over a trading post on the Menominee River. Marie would prove valuable to the business since she could speak multiple languages. Eventually, she and Jacobs split, and she and Farnsworth would marry.

Her role in the business grew, and she became a respected businesswoman and Marinette resident. Farnsworth would eventually leave and head south, making his home in Sheboygan, while Marie would take over the business on her own. In a virtually unheard of scenario in the 1800's, 'Queen Marinette' competed in a man's world and earned equal regard.

Red Arrow Park

Marinette has several parks to enjoy. A favorite is Red Arrow Park on the Bay of Green Bay. This extensive park has a monument that pays tribute to Marinette military veterans, a beach, playground, rentable pavilion, picnic areas, and trails. This is where you can access the Seagull Bar, a Wisconsin State Natural Area.

Seagull Bar is the only true dune complex on the Bay of Green Bay. According to the Wisconsin DNR, the area is 120 acres, and was named a State Nature Area in 1962. It is a migratory bird staging area, making it one of the best places to birdwatch. The shallow waters in the lagoon are home to waterfowl and many species of wetland plants. The walk out and back is about 2.6 miles, but that can vary depending upon the bay water levels and wave action.

Another trail within Red Arrow Park is the Menekaunee Nature Path, which is a short walk along the marshy area of the park. This small stretch is excellent for birdwatching and viewing other wildlife. I have spotted white-tailed deer walking on the path.

On the beach side of the park, you will see the Menekaunee Restoration Walking Path. This trail runs from Red Arrow Park to Menekaunee Harbor. This is a paved trail making it accessible to everyone. The trail includes a footbridge to cross the Menominee River to enter Menekaunee Harbor Park.

318 East Bayshore Street

Menekaunee Harbor and Park

This park is a newer addition to Marinette. It was part of a large improvement project that included cleaning up the river and adding a state-of-the-art harbor facility. The harbor now has pavilions, three boat slips, a restroom building, and an accessible kayak launch. You will also see many statues and art installations celebrating Marinette's fishing heritage.

The spotlight in the Menekaunee Harbor Park is the tall bear statue at the edge of the park. This bear honors the first settlement of the Menominee Indian Tribe on the banks of the Menominee River. Coming in at almost 14 feet, this is a replica of the ancestral bear that is at the Menominee Tribe's Cultural Museum in Keshena, Wisconsin. The five spotlights that illuminate the bear signify the five different clans of the Menominee Tribe. While it's great to pay a visit to the harbor during the day, I would suggest a drive over to see this majestic statue at night.

In 2019, the city published a comprehensive 5-year plan to improve outdoor recreation in the city with the addition of more all-use trails, bike paths, and general maintenance to existing park facilities. (Photo page 241)

Ogden Street

Mariner Movie Theater

If you're yearning for a bit of retro nostalgia, catch a movie at the Mariner Movie Theater. It keeps its original 60s vibe with state-of-the-art visual and audio experience. The Mariner runs second run movies for $4. The seats are comfy and there are tables in front of you to set your pizza, hot dogs, and slurpees and on. Go early to spend some time playing the 80s arcade games in the lobby.

2000 Ella Ct.

marinertheater.com

Shopping

Seguin's Cheese

For cheese and so much more, stop in at Seguin's Cheese. It's just minutes from downtown and is brimming with gifts, clothing, everything you need for a picnic at Red Arrow Park, and souvenirs to bring home. There's also a full line of Minnetonka Moccasins.

W1968 US Hwy 41

seguinscheese.com

Main Street Antique Mall

This Is a great stop to find interesting items. The store comprises booths rented to individuals, so each booth has its own personality, dependent on what the owners' interests are. Some booths have their own well-designed theme, while others are just an eclectic mix of items. Either way, it's fun to explore. Don't miss going upstairs to the **Studio B Art Gallery** featuring the works of local artist **Rusty Wolfe.** Where else can you find a contemporary art gallery inside an antique mall?

1622 Main Street

mainstreetantiquemalls.com

rustywolfe.com

Simply Charming Boutique

Simply Charming Boutique is also located inside the historic Lauerman's Department store. Along with affordable fashion, you can find accessories, furniture and gifts.

1713 Dunlap Avenue

Phone: 715) 732-9300

The Goose and Gander Finery

Also inside Lauerman's Department store, this fun shop has an eclectic mix of clothing, cards, baby and kid's things, jewelry and accessories, along with gift items and home goods. It's a great place to grab a special gift to bring home.

1712 Dunlap Avenue

gooseandganderfinery.com

Places to eat and drink in Marinette

Coffee and Bakery

Zinger Coffee & Tea

Voted best coffee shop in the area. Great drive-up coffee shop that offers all kinds of specialty drinks along with scones and other grab and go items. Seasonal lattes and cappuccinos include Pistachio Dream and spiced Toffee Nut.

1739 Marinette Avenue

Phone: (715) 732-5454

A Place For Coffee

With a personality as tall as the ceilings in this former church, this is a great place to sit and enjoy your coffee, read the paper, and get some work done. There's a variety of muffins and other bakery items, plus, it offers sugar-free options and a vast variety of syrups for your coffee. Try my favorite specialty latte, a Peanut Butter Cup. Owner Jen Schiller and her staff are very welcoming and you'll feel right at home.

1059 Marinette Avenue

Phone: (715) 330-6191

Restaurants

Hometown Family Restaurant

Serves breakfast, lunch and dinner. If you are in the mood for hometown cooking, this is for you. The breakfasts are excellent. And don't forget the pie. Have it there or ask for a slice to go. Definitely where the locals go!

1400 Marinette Avenue

Phone: (715) 735-3640

Cafe' Green

If you're looking for a fresh and healthy alternative to fast food, Cafe Green is a tasty choice. Offering sandwiches, salads, wraps, and flatbread pizzas. Open for lunch only.

1633 Main Street

thecafegreen.com

Blue Bike Burrito

Another great choice for lunch. Simple menu offering burritos, tacos, quesadillas, and nachos. Only open for lunch.

2020 Hall Avenue

bluebikeburrito.com

Applejack's Restaurant & Pub

Open for breakfast, lunch and dinner. Breakfast, burgers, pizza, seafood, and chicken.

20 West Hosmer Street

Phone: (715) 732-4772

Mickey-Lu-BBQ

Iconic old-style diner with counter and table seating. I suggest everyone who visits Marinette stops at Mickey-Lu at least once. Old-fashioned prices and a simple menu of burgers, brats, hot dogs, and grilled cheese all made over the grill right in front of you. Take my word for it and have a chocolate malt with your burger. Because of the small and usually crowded interior, it's common to experience a bit of a wait.

1710 Marinette Avenue

Phone: (715) 735-7721

Railhouse Restaurant & Brewpub

Railhouse has a large menu with a variety of food. Pasta, Mexican, fish, and chicken. There's something for everyone. And for beer drinkers, there are eleven house brews on tap.

2029 Old Peshtigo Court

railhousebrewpub.com

Tastebuds Smokehouse & Spirits

In the same building as the Exxon Gas Station, you might just miss Tastebuds except for the full parking lot and people coming in and out of the restaurant.

Open all day from breakfast till dinner and offering tasty BBQ and a popular Friday Fish Fry.

2680 Cleveland Avenue

tastebudssmokehouse.com

La Cabana Mexican Cuisine

If Mexican food is what you're looking for in a great authentic atmosphere, La Cabana is your best option. Everything is wonderful. It's a fun place to go with family and friends. The margaritas are sensational. Open for lunch and dinner. Happy Hour Monday through Thursday 2 pm - 5 pm.

1553 Marinette Avenue

lacabanamexicancuisine.com

Ironworks on Main

Even if you don't stop to eat here, you must look up at the top of the building to see artist Sergio Furnari's life-sized sculptures depicting eleven workers eating lunch on a steel beam during construction of Rockefeller Center. The inspiration for this installation comes from the popular 1932 photograph.

Inside the restaurant, you get a blue-collar industrial feel. Ironworks serves lunch and dinner in this historic building.

1333 Main Street

Phone: (715) 504-2000

Brothers Three

Brothers Three boasts it has the "best pizza in town." You'll have to be the judge. Open for lunch and dinner and a wide variety of food on the menu.

1302 Marinette Avenue

thebrothersthree.com

Bars, Wineries, and Breweries

Forgotten Fire Winery

Stop in for a tasting of excellent wines that are produced in house. Tastings cost $5 for seven samples and the glass is yours to keep. There is ample seating to enjoy a glass or two once you decide on your favorite. Purchase a bottle to take home with you.

The winery opened in 2011. Original owners Joe and Lindsey Callow named their winery "Forgotten Fire" after the Peshtigo Fire, which happened on October 8, 1871, the same day as the great Chicago Fire, hence the "forgotten" part. The current owners, Chris and Melissa Joppe, continue to honor that history today.

N2393 Schacht Road

forgottenfirewinery.com

Accommodations

Hotels and Bed and Breakfast

Baymont by Wyndham Marinette

Formerly Comfort Inn. Free parking, Wi-Fi, and free breakfast. Fitness and business centers are available.

2180 Roosevelt Road

wyndhamhotels.com

Country Inn and Suites by Radisson

Comfortable clean rooms. Free parking, Wi-Fi, and breakfast. Pool and fitness room. Kitchenette with a refrigerator and microwave.

2020 Old Peshtigo Ct

radissonhotelsamericas.com

Lauerman

House Inn

Gorgeous bed and breakfast on historic Riverside Drive. Local business owner Joseph A Lauerman, along with his brothers Charles and Frank, built this historic home in 1910. They opened the Lauerman Brothers Department Store in downtown Marinette the same year.

Today, the home offers seven guest rooms with private bathrooms. The house has kept some of its original character with detailed wood trim and original chandeliers.

1975 Riverside Avenue

mmvictorian.com

M&M Victorian Inn

A lumber baron built the Queen Anne style home in 1893 as a wedding gift to his daughter. Beautiful leaded stained glass windows, rich woodwork, and original pocket doors, along with fun and funky retro touches, give this historic home a new twist and unpredictable flavor. There are five guest rooms with private bathrooms. Also onsite is 1393 Lounge Martini & Dessert Bar, which draws visitors from around the world who are in town for business or pleasure.

1393 Main Street

mmvictorian.com

Campgrounds

City Park Campground

Small campground right in the city with nine sites, 20 amp service, bathroom and shower facilities. There is potable water available, but no dump site. You can make reservations at the Community REC Center at 2501 Pierce Avenue.

1905 Hall Avenue

Phone: (715) 732-2006

River Park Campground

Just across the bridge on US Highway 41 and on the Menominee River in Michigan is the busy River Park Campground. There are 58 paved sites, most with full hookups. Nightly rates run from $20 for a tent site to $40 for a prime river site with full hookups. Bathroom and shower facilities are available and the dump station is located outside the fenced area. The main boat landing is next to the campground, along with a fish cleaning station. Within walking distance to shopping and restaurants.

1401 8TH Ave Menominee, Michigan

Phone: (906) 863-5101

Ashland

Ashland, Wisconsin, is best known for its many mural paintings that line the buildings of the historic downtown. Within these murals, visitors learn about the people and places that tell the history of Ashland. Some come to admire the artistic beauty of the murals, some to learn about Ashland's interesting history. Every visitor comes away with an appreciation of both.

While the primary draw to Ashland is these murals, Ashland offers so much more.

Ashland is the first Wisconsin Harbor Town on Lake Superior. I have always had a major soft spot for Lake Superior and have spent many a summer vacation on its shores. Ashland is a vibrant, yet charming destination, where it's easy to spend a weekend discovering its many merits.

Location

US Highway 2 is the major way to get to Ashland. If you are going from harbor town to harbor town, the driving distance from Marinette to Ashland is over 4 hours and there are multiple routes to take. You really cannot go wrong with whichever route you choose. The shortest routes will take you on a scenic drive through Wisconsin's north woods with an abundance of small towns to discover on the way.

You could also choose the long route through Michigan's Upper Peninsula. Take Highway 35 north out of Marinette and drive up the Bay of Green Bay coastline until Escanaba and cut across on Highway 41 till you hit US Highway 2. This will add roughly an hour onto your drive.

Ashland Facts

- The Ojibwe Native American tribe first inhabited Ashland before French fur traders arrived in the area in the 17th century.

- The city was officially founded in 1887 during a period of rapid growth and development in northern Wisconsin, fueled by the logging industry.

- Ashland played a key role in the shipping and transport of lumber during the late 19th and early 20th centuries because of its location on the shores of Lake Superior.

- In the early 1900s, the city became a center for commercial fishing and home to a large Finnish population.

- Today, Ashland has a population of 7,918 (2021)

How Much Time To Spend In Ashland

Visitors can easily spend a weekend in Ashland. It's also a great home base to explore the entire area. While it's quiet in winter, from late spring through fall, the area is bursting with fun things to do and see. It's all about enjoying the outdoors.

Things To Do In Ashland

Highlights

ASHLAND

The shore of Lake Superior is the focal point as you're driving through Ashland. We will look at some places that take advantage of that stunning Lake Superior coastline.

Lighthouse

Ashland Breakwater Lighthouse-This lighthouse began its service in 1915 at the end of a man-made breakwater. It had seven different keepers until its automation in 1962. Today Breakwater Lighthouse shines brightly and is a part of the National Park Service's Apostle Island National Lakeshore. It is not open to the public and you can only get close enough to observe the water.

Historic Murals of Ashland

One of the major visitor attractions in Ashland is the mural artwork that lines the downtown area. These 23 historic murals tell the story of Ashland's culture and history. You can take a self-guided tour using the Historic Murals of Ashland guide available downtown at the Ashland Area Chamber of Commerce, or available online at their website. In summer, you can go on a trolley tour to see the murals. Most of the murals are contained in an eight-block stretch of the downtown business district that is listed in the National Register of Historic Places, so I suggest taking a walk as the best way to see them. (Photo page 294)

Murals can be seen at various locations around the city.

Ashland Historical Society Museum

If you're in the mood for more of Ashland's history, stop in at the Ashland Historical Society Museum in the middle of downtown. There are displays with historical artifacts, along with a gift shop. It's worth an hour if you want to learn more about Ashland's ore dock, its workers, and the railroad.

216 Main Street West

ashlandwishistory.com

David R. Obey Northern Great Lakes Visitor Center

Two miles west of Ashland is the David R. Obey Northern Great Lakes Visitors Center. There is much more here than just a visitors' center. You must head up to the five-story observation tower. On the way up, you will see the 18th mural called 'The Community Of Life: Our Evolving Relationship with the Land." It is a timeline mural demonstrating human impact on the local ecosystem. The tower showcases stunning views of the Whittlesey National Wildlife Refuge to the north.

The center hosts various events throughout the year. If you feel the need to stretch your legs, take a walk along the trails around the visitor center.

29270 CO Highway G

nglvc.org

Waterfront Trail

There are two not-to-be-missed gems in Ashland. One is the Waterfront Trail, an 11.5 mile paved trail that mostly runs along the Lake Superior shoreline. This Rails-to-Trails path takes you past seven city parks, public artworks, beaches, an accessible pier, and a connection to the historic center. The trail is open to bikers, walkers, and runners and is ADA compliant. You can find a PDF map of the entire trail on the Visit Ashland website.

Prentice Park

My second gem is Prentice Park. Because this park is not visible from the highway, visitors often overlook it. It is on the western end of Ashland. You can get to it by turning onto Turner Road off of Highway 2. It is Ashland's largest park at 100 acres. There are a handful of first come, first served campsites that are really nice. There are walking trails with a boardwalk, restrooms, an artesian well, pavilions, and a playground. I loved parking here and walking the boardwalk. It is peaceful and the marshy area is ideal for birdwatching. It's a great place to start your walk along the Waterfront Trail.

Park Road

coawi.org/381/Campgrounds

Maslowski Park

Maslowski Park is across from Prentice Park on Lake Superior. In the summer, this park is busy with travelers stopping to take a swim in the cool lake at the beach area. This is also a popular spot to fill up your water at the artesian well you can find inside a cute little structure. You also have access to the Waterfront Trail here. The park has restrooms, a playground, pavilion, and a volleyball net. (Photo page 294)

Lake Shore Drive West

visitashland.com/directory/maslowski-beach

Kreher Park

Next along the Waterfront Trail is Kreher Park. This park is near the Ashland Marina and has a boat landing, beach, pier, bathhouse, and a pavilion. There is a good-sized, first come, first served campground here.

200 Prentice Avenue North

coawi.org/381/Campgrounds

Bayview Park

Bayview Park is one of the best parks in Ashland. It's in this park that you'll find the newest pier and at the end of that pier, you'll find a diving board where the daring can plunge into the crisp waters of Lake Superior. There's a sizable beach here, too. When I visited, there were a few people flying kites along the beach. It's here you can get a glimpse of the Ashland Breakwater Lighthouse, which is only accessible by boat.

1543-1783 Lake Shore Drive East

visitashland.com/directory/bayview-beach

Pearson Plaza Park

Now let's move away from the lakeshore to downtown. The newest park in Ashland is Pearson Plaza Park. It's best to see it when the flowers are in full bloom. I was delighted to stumble upon this park during my Ashland adventures. Plus, it leads to my favorite discovery in Ashland.

Behind City Hall

Ed Griffiths Pedestrian Pass

My favorite thing in Ashland is the Ed Griffiths Pedestrian Pass, which is a tunnel that runs underneath Highway 2 and connects downtown to the Waterfront Trail. What's so special about this tunnel?

This painted tunnel is a communitywide project that features delightful mosaic animals and plants done by community groups and school children. The painted landscape depicts the ecology of the area.

601 Main Street West, or 6th Avenue West Beach

visitashland.com/25528-2

Things To Do Near Ashland

Nearby **Copper Falls State Park** covers over 3,000 acres and includes several miles of hiking trails. These trails offer varying degrees of difficulty, so there's something for everyone from casual walkers to experienced hikers. The park's principal attraction is its three waterfalls. They can be viewed from several vantage points. One of the most popular is the 40-foot Copper Falls, which can be reached via a short walk from the main parking area. The park also includes a series of cascading waterfalls and rapids along the Bad River, which can be viewed from several hiking trails.

Besides the waterfalls, the park offers plenty of opportunities for other outdoor activities like fishing, swimming, and camping. People know the Bad River for its excellent fishing, with trout, bass, and other species that people can find in its waters.

You shouldn't miss Copper Falls State Park, a great side trip from Ashland. The park is located two miles northeast of Mellen on Highway 169. It takes about 35 minutes to get there from Ashland.

The other spot to view a waterfall is Morgan Falls. Morgan Falls is about 30 minutes from Ashland. The hike to this 70 foot falls is about a half mile. The hike to Morgan Falls is easy to moderate, and the trail is well maintained. It's surrounded by lush forests and is a perfect destination for a hike and picnic. If you want more of a challenge, you can continue up to St. Peter's Dome, which is a scenic overlook that offers panoramic views of the surrounding forests and lakes. It is roughly 2 miles one way, and the trail is rugged, peppered with exposed rocks and steep slopes.

A daily pass is $5, and there is a self-pay station in the parking lot.

Shopping

For a town of Ashland's size, there are more than enough shopping opportunities here. Most of the retail businesses line the historic Main Street area, or just a block off the street, so doing a little retail therapy along with the Mural Walk is an excellent way to spend an afternoon.

Gabriele's German Cookies and Chocolate

You must stop at Gabriele's. It's hard to miss this enchanting candy store - with its gingerbread house facade complete with Hansel and Gretel painted on the front (painted by muralist Sue Martinsen).

Walking inside, you will be overcome with the sweet smells of delectable confections coming from the kitchen. If you're lucky, Gabriele will come out and share her story with you. The day I visited I was the only one in the store, so I could chat with her and her husband, David. I was quickly enamored with them, but my attention was being pulled toward the glass case with some of the most beautiful truffles I have ever seen.

Gabriele was born in Germany and has fond memories of Christmas celebrated in the traditional German way. Everything is handmade in her shop and many of the recipes are passed down from family.

The specialty cookies are to die for, not to mention the truffles. My biggest regret leaving Ashland was forgetting to bring the cookies I bought, leaving them behind in the room refrigerator.

413 Main Street West

gabrielesgermansweets.com

Red Bicycle Gift Shoppe

This is one of those shops you can lose yourself in. Part vintage resale, part reimagined items, and all fun unique decor. It takes a while to really see everything and I can almost bet you will find at least one thing that you absolutely have to bring home. I love shopping for vintage things, and if you do too, you'll have to stop here.

618 West Main Street

Solstice Clothing and Goods

This adorable shop has fun ladies' fashions and accessories along with gift items. It's affiliated with **Solstice Outdoors,** which is the outfitter on the edge of town (2521 West Lake Shore Drive) on Lake Superior. Along with outdoor retail goods, you can rent bikes, paddleboards, canoes and skis and snowshoes in winter.

400 Main Street West

solsticeoutdoorstore.com

A 2nd Look

Ashland has some great consignment/resale shops and this is my favorite. It's packed with name brand clothing and accessories set up in a clean and organized space. You'll also find some furniture and housewares.

311 W. Main Street

The Union Boutique LLC

Classy, upscale women's clothing boutique inside the historic Union Bank.

100 Main Street West

theunionashland.com

The Shelter Shop

This resale shop features furniture, housewares, and home decor. Proceeds go to the Chequamegon Humane Society.

216 & 218 4th Ave West

Touch Of The North

Home decor, jewelry, and gifts

715 Main Street West

Places To Eat And Drink In Ashland

Coffee and Bakery

Black Cat Coffeehouse

The favorite place in Ashland to sit and sip your latte is definitely Black Cat Coffeehouse. It was clearly once a bar, but is now transformed into a community gathering place with tables in the front and cozy seating areas with fully stocked bookshelves in the back room. In summer, the coffeehouse hosts concerts on the back patio. You can grab breakfast and lunch here too. The ingredients are locally sourced, and the coffee comes from nearby Duluth. Black Cat also offers tea, smoothies, and more.

211 Chapple Avenue

blackcatashland.com

Ashland Baking Company

When you've had your coffee, cross the street and sample some bakery treats here. This is a must stop! Even when I was in neighboring Bayfield, I had people tell me not to miss this bakery. It did not disappoint. I ordered a piece of cheesecake to go. Delicious. Almond cake, brownies, bread, you can't go wrong.

212 Chapple Avenue

ashlandbakingcompany.com

Restaurants

Deepwater Grille and The Alley

These restaurants are next to each other on Main Street. Deepwater Grill is fine dining with pub food. It's also a brew pub called South Shore Brewery. They brew five flagship varieties that are available all year, along with specialty and seasonal brews.

Next door, The Alley is famous for its Brick Oven pizza, but also serves burgers, wings, and more.

808 Main Street West

deepwatergrille.com

The Local Bar and Grille

This restaurant is at the Chequamegon Golf Club on the western end of Ashland. It serves up American fare, burgers, steak, sandwiches, and salads. The restaurant also has weekly specials such as all-you-can-eat Friday Fish Fry and Prime Rib Saturdays. Open seven days a week for lunch and dinner.

3000 Golf Course Road

thelocalbarandgrille.com

Accommodations

Hotels

Cobblestone Inn and Suites

Ashland's newest hotel right in the middle of town and within walking distance to everything. It's clean, modern, with kitchenettes. Accessible rooms, pet-friendly, and breakfast included. I loved staying here for its access to everything downtown.

818 Main Street West

staycobblestone.com/wi/ashland

Blue Wave Inn

This is an elegant, five-room boutique inn on Chequamegon Bay. All rooms face the bay for a relaxing experience. Each room has a mini fridge and a coffee maker. It's connected to Solstice Outdoors, so you have kayak and paddleboard and bike rentals right there. It's also right on the Waterfront Trail.

2521 West Lake Shore Drive

.bluewaveinnashland.com

The Inn at Timber Cove

If you are looking for the ultimate peaceful setting, a bit of history, and your own private guest cottage, this is perfect for you. There are three guest cottages on this property, just a mile from the lakeshore. Each cottage can sleep two guests.

1319 Sanborn Avenue

innattimbercove.com

Campgrounds

Prentice Park and Kreher Park

I mentioned the first come, first served campsites at Prentice Park and Kreher Park. You can call (715) 682-7059 for availability at either park the same day or after 9:30 am. Prentice Park has six primitive tent sites and seven RV sites with electricity and water onsite. There is also a shower house and restrooms.

Kreher Park has 33 RV sites with water and electricity.

coawi.org

Copper Falls State Park

Copper Falls has two campgrounds on the property. The South Campground is entirely non- electric camping with some walk-in sites. The North Campground has 32 sites of which 28 are electric, and one accessible campsite across from the restrooms. There is also one rustic cabin and one backpack site. Reservations can be made online.

dnr.wisconsin.gov/topic/parks/copperfalls

Washburn

Washburn is known as "The Little Town on the Big Lake." Most travelers drive right through Washburn on their way to Bayfield without stopping, but I think Washburn deserves attention and a little exploration. There are three historic brownstone buildings on the National Register of Historic Places, beaches, arts and culture, and then some great food options just waiting for travelers to discover.

Location

Washburn is a simple drive from Ashland, just 11 miles north on Highway 13. It's almost smack in the middle between Ashland and Bayfield.

Washburn Facts

- Washburn's founders established it in the late 19th century. Its location significantly influenced its development on Lake Superior because of the logging industry. There were three sawmills operating in Washburn until the early 20th century.

- Washburn is home to the Bayfield County seat.

- Post-logging era, Washburn underwent a transition from a logging-based economy to more diversified industries, including fishing, and more recently, tourism.

- Many buildings in downtown Washburn reflect the architectural styles of the late 19th and early 20th centuries, indicative of the town's historical prosperity during the logging boom. Construction of many of these historical buildings utilized the "Apostle Brownstone" quarried in the area. These structures often serve as physical reminders of the town's rich past.

- Today Washburn's population is 2,055 (2021)

How Much Time To Spend In Washburn

I would suggest spending a day if you want to hit the highlights in Washburn. With its location between Ashland and Bayfield, you can certainly make Washburn your home base if you only have a long weekend or a week to explore the entire area.

Things To Do In Washburn

I suggest you stop at the Washburn Area Chamber building when you arrive in town. You will find important information about events happening during your visit. You can also pick up a map to take the Washburn Historic Buildings Tour.

Washburn Highlights

Washburn Historic Buildings Tour

This self-guided tour takes you to nine stops in town. You can see architecture and fine examples of buildings made from local brownstone quarried in the Apostle Island area. Pick up a map before you begin your tour at the Washburn Area Chamber building.

100 West Bayfield Street

washburnchamber.com

Washburn Cultural Center

This center, housed in one of the historic buildings on the Washburn Historic Buildings Tour, showcases local art, history, and cultural exhibits. There's a museum inside dedicated to local artifacts and history and a gift shop with souvenirs. Make sure you visit the website for hours.

1 East Bayfield Street

washburnculturalcenter.com/work

Catch A Show At StageNorth Theater

StageNorth Groundlings is the local production company that puts on shows ranging from creative original shows to theatrical and Broadway hits.

123 West Omaha Street

stagenorth.com

Washburn Lakeshore Parkway and Walking Trail

This trail, which stretches over a mile and runs along the Lake Superior shoreline, is a popular spot for walkers and hikers. There are three beaches you can access for a dip in the cool lake waters. It's moderate in ability and there is a section that is wheelchair friendly. Park in West End Park and access the trail from there. The trail runs to the marina and farther into Memorial Park.

Enjoy A Cool Drink Of Water From An Artesian Well

There are two artesian wells at West End Park for you to quench your thirst. You'll see locals come to fill up water jugs with the pure water.

Thompson's West End Park

Shopping

Chequamegon Books

What's more enticing than the scent of books? This bookstore has a collection of new, used, and discounted books. With more than 70,000 books in its inventory, you may find that rare addition you've been looking for. You can cozy up with a cup of coffee too.

2 East Bayfield Street

chequamegonbooks.com

ABC Thrift Stores

You know I love thrifting and ABC Thrift is a gem! The prices are fantastic but bring cash. The store does not accept credit cards. If you're lucky, you'll be there for one of the store's bag sales.

118 East Bayfield Street

Phone: (715) 373-5929

Harbor House Sweets

Who doesn't love an adorable small town candy shop? Bring a box home for a friend of specially handmade Lake Superior chocolates, or indulge in homemade ice cream and sorbets in the summer. Owner Ginamarie brings a passion for baking and candy making to Washburn.

127 West Bayfield Street

harborhousesweets.com

Ghost Ship Gallery

This artist collective has nine studios and an impressive eclectic gallery space that features the work of over 50 artists from the surrounding community. Did I mention you can also grab a local brew while you soak in the inspirational vibes? This is a must-stop for anyone who appreciates the arts.

318 West Bayfield Street

ghostshipgallery.com

Places To Eat And Drink In Washburn

Coffee and Bakery

Cafe Coco

This bakery and eatery is quite famous in the area. In fact, I sampled the bread when I was staying in Bayfield and was won over! I knew I had to stop. But woman cannot live by bread alone, so owner Noreen offers a delectable array of pastries and desserts, all made from scratch. Her menu offers breakfast, lunch, deli options, and custom cakes, with a focus on accommodating various dietary preferences including gluten-free, vegan, and vegetarian options. Definitely a must-stop.

146 West Bayfield Street

coconorth.com

Patsy's Bar & Grill

Patsy's has been a local favorite for over 30 years, specializing in classic American comfort food. They are renowned for their burgers, which were voted the Best in Bayfield County in 2014 and 2017. The menu also features a popular Friday Fish Fry, sandwiches, soups, and salads, all made with fresh, high-quality ingredients. The restaurant has a welcoming atmosphere with a full-service bar, occasional live music, and a seasonal patio. Don't be surprised if it's busy, since it's one of the local gathering spots.

328 West Bayfield Street

patsysbarandgrill.com

The Fat Radish

This restaurant, known for its cozy and eclectic ambiance, offers a unique farm-to-table dining experience. The menu is quite diverse, featuring American, Indian, Thai, and seafood cuisines, along with Gluten-Free and vegetarian options. Customers have particularly enjoyed dishes like Roasted Vegetables, Eggs Benedict, Lamb Shank, Fish Fry, and Mac. The Fat Radish caters to various dietary needs, making it a suitable choice for a wide range of visitors. The Fat Radish was previously located in nearby Cornucopia.

905 West Bayfield Street

thefatradish.weebly.com

DaLou's Bistro

A local favorite for Italian cuisine, DaLou's Bistro serves delicious wood-fired pizza and offers a cozy dining experience. If you're not a pizza fan, you can also get pasta dishes. Try the homemade gelato.

310 West Bayfield Street

dalousbistro.com

Good Thyme Restaurant & Catering

This restaurant offers artisan cuisine with generous portions in a historic (built in 1898) yellow home. The wrap-around veranda speaks of old time elegance. They are known for their steak, whitefish, and pork shank dishes, as well as a notable brown butter cake dessert. The restaurant has a Friday Fish Fry at night.

77180 State Highway 13

goodthyme.catering

Bars, Wineries, and Breweries

South Shore Brewery

The main South Shore Brewery production is right here in Washburn. If you're thirsty and want to try the brews, there is a taphouse located here. You can order food from a list of local eateries, bring it in and enjoy your beer. I really like the award-winning Nut Brown Ale.

532 West Bayfield

southshorebrewery.com

Sweet Treats

Harbor House Sweets

See above.

Accommodations

There's not a lot to choose from as far as accommodations go in Washburn. For this reason, you may make Ashland or Bayfield your home base. There are some rental properties available, as well as a few hotels. Here are my suggestions.

Hotels

The Washburn Inn

The Washburn Inn is known for its clean and comfortable rooms, friendly staff, and a lakeside setting. Guests can choose from a variety of room types including Double Queen, Single Queen, and King Suite, all recently renovated with modern amenities. The hotel also features facilities for disabled guests, free WiFi, free parking, and beachfront access. Nearby, guests can enjoy activities like kayaking on Lake Superior, exploring the Apostle Islands, or attending concerts at the Big Top Chautauqua. For dining, the Harbor Table restaurant offers delightful meals next to the hotel.

128 Harbor View Drive

washburninn.com

Campgrounds

Memorial Park Campground

This city park campground offers sites on a first come, first served basis. They have 50 total sites that are available daily, weekly, and 14 sites, seasonally. All the sites are in a wooded area, some lakeside. There is a dump site, a playground, and most sites have electricity. Because this campground is wooded, it is best for smaller RVs and tent camping.

cityofwashburn.org

Thompson's West End Park

If you have a larger RV and appreciate sunny camping, then camping in Thompson's West End Park is a better choice versus Memorial Park. This campground is also first come, first served, and has a swimming beach, playground, and boat launch. West End has 50 electric sites, 17 of them are seasonal. There is also a dump station available. You'll also find pay showers and flush toilets.

cityofwashburn.org

Birch Grove Campground

Camping here is primitive, with no electric hookups or flush toilets. Tucked between East Twin Lake and West Twin Lake, Birch Lake Campground is equipped with 16 campsites, each featuring a parking spur, fire ring, picnic table, and tent pad. It can accommodate RVs up to 35 feet. The campground has no reservation system and operates on a first come, first served basis.

Forest Road 435

fs.usda.gov/recarea/cnnf/recreation/camping-cabins/recarea/?recid=27831&actid=29

Bayfield

As you drive into Bayfield, a rush of excitement courses through your veins. The scene before you is straight out of a postcard, and you can't believe your eyes. The shimmering blue waters of Lake Superior stretch out before you. Your gaze wanders over to the harbor, where majestic sailboats sway gently in the breeze. You can feel the cool air on your face and smell the tangy scent of the lake. As you look up the hillside, you see an array of charming cottages nestled among grandiose Victorian homes. It feels like you've stumbled upon a secret gem hidden away on the East Coast, but no–this is Wisconsin, and you're filled with awe at the beauty that surrounds you.

Bayfield may be the smallest city in Wisconsin, but it is super-sized in charm. It's the docking point to the Apostle Islands National Lakeshore, and it's a destination that calls to visitors from around the world each year.

It may be a popular tourist destination, but I love Bayfield for its history, quaint feel, and many outdoor delights. You can easily spend a summer vacation week in Bayfield and never be bored.

Location

Bayfield is our next Wisconsin Harbor Town after Washburn on Lake Superior. From Washburn, you continue north on Highway 13, for about 16 minutes, which will take you right into the center of Bayfield.

Bayfield Facts

- Bayfield was established in 1856, two years after the final Land Cession Treaty between the US and the Ojibwe was signed.

- Bayfield is named after Henry Wolsey Bayfield, who surveyed Lake Superior during 1823-1825.

- Early industry was logging, fishing, and quarrying the brownstone seen in many of the buildings in the area.

- Bayfield has a population of 588 (2021). Today, in order to earn city status, a place must have a population of at least 1000 people.

- A 50 block area of Bayfield is listed on the National Register of Historic Places.

- Today, tourism is the primary industry of Bayfield.

A visitor can easily spend a long weekend in Bayfield. Summer is the best time to visit, but winter has gained popularity in recent years with visitors coming to see the famous Ice Caves along the Apostle Islands National Shoreline.

Things To Do In Bayfield

Bayfield is a bustling town from late May through September when the tourist season is in high gear. Many local businesses open seasonally, and some only on certain days, so be sure to check days and times before making a special trip to visit these places.

Bayfield Highlights

Stop at the **Bayfield Visitors Center** at 42 S Broad Street for more information and maps about the following things I mention here.

Lighthouses

There are no lighthouses in Bayfield, but the Apostle Islands National Lakeshore has several in the area. There are two that are open in season for ranger guided tours. You can access them by private water taxi, or Apostle Island Cruises (website and address listed below).

Raspberry Island Lighthouse- Raspberry Island Lighthouse began service in 1863. The builders constructed a boxy-shaped two-bedroom dwelling for the keeper around the light tower. In 1906, they determined that the current structure of the original lighthouse could not accommodate three keepers. It underwent extensive renovation. It appears much the same way it did then. The light was automated in 1947. The Wisconsin State Historical Society Museum on Madeline Island displays that original lens.

nps.gov/apis/learn/historyculture/raspberry-light.htm

Old Michigan Lighthouse- Michigan Island is 17 miles from Bayfield, making it fairly remote. Construction began on the lighthouse in 1856. It was tough going. The materials, including the stone, had to be brought by boat. In 1958, the lighthouse was shut down until the lens was replaced in 1868 and the lighthouse was reopened.

In 1929, a new tower was built for more visibility. After a series of keepers came and went, the light was automated in 1943. Today the National Park Service works to maintain the site so visitors can learn about the lighthouse and the keepers who lived their lives on this remote island.

Tour Bayfield's Fruit Loop

Bayfield's climate makes it the perfect spot to grow fruit, and there is no shortage of farms and orchards in the area. In the summer, grab a map of the local orchards at the Bayfield Visitors Center and drive the Fruit Loop. There are 14 stops, including orchards, farms, and wineries. You can easily spend a day visiting them all. The three-day Bayfield Apple Festival draws enormous crowds every October and is the biggest event in town.

There are 51 varieties of apples grown in the Bayfield area, with blueberries and pears guest stars at the orchards. In fact, you will find jams, baked goods, strawberries and other fresh produce on the Fruit Loop.

One of my favorite stops on the loop is **Garage Mahal Orchard**. This orchard is solely blueberries. Why make a special stop here when you can find blueberries at the other orchards? The blueberries are so yummy, but the real draw to Garage Mahal Orchard is its owner, Michael Berg. Originally from Germany, he worked for Honeywell and 3M in the arts department. He became a fan of the Bayfield area after spending fishing trips here. In 1971, he moved to Bayfield after his retirement and started the blueberry hobby farm to employ Native Americans in the area. That's still his mission today. Raising blueberries and helping the locals is a labor of love for him.

Don't miss **Hauser's Superior View Farm**. The big red barn catches your eye when you drive in. Inside that barn is a store selling produce, flowers, jams, butters, caramel apples and local souvenirs. Here you can also taste test some of that fine Apfelhaus Cider.

If you're a wine drinker, stop at **Bayfield Winery and Blue Ox Cider**. I love the wine made here, from local fruit. Taste test a flight to see which one you like best. In summer, grab a bottle of wine and sit outside to enjoy live music on Saturdays.

Explore the Apostle Islands and Sea Caves

Bayfield is the stepping off point to the Apostle Islands National Lakeshore. The park consists of 22 islands; Madeline Island being the largest.

If you are adventurous and an experienced sea kayaker, there are kayaking tours available through local outfitters. Doing one of these tours is not a leisurely paddle along a quiet river. The lake conditions can change drastically, making kayaking hazardous for the inexperienced.

For a list of places that offer kayaking tours, use this URL on the National Park Service website: https://www.nps.gov/apis/planyourvisit/commercial-services.htm

While I like to kayak, I prefer the other method of seeing the islands. That would be an **Apostle Island Cruises** boat ride. They offer several tours, from an overall Grand Tour and lighthouse tours, to overnight camping on Oak or Stockton Island. The Grand Tour is available three times daily June through September. You'll get a view of the Strawberry and Devils Island Lighthouses, a fishing camp, and what I see as the feature of the tour, the sea caves on Devils Island. Advance reservations are encouraged.

Apostle Island Cruises

2 Front Street

apostleisland.com

Bayfield Maritime Museum

This free museum (donations accepted) contains artifacts, boats, and other items pertaining to the maritime history of the area. It's worth an hour if you are interested in the local history.

131 South 1st Street

bayfieldmaritimemuseum.org

Catch A Show At Big Top Chautauqua

For over 35 years, Big Top Chautauqua has been bringing in headline and local entertainment for residents and visitors to this part of Wisconsin. What's cooler than filling your summer nights with music, comedy, and special presentations under the big top with the stars shimmering overhead?

32525 Ski Hill Road

bigtop.org

Beaver Hollow Nature Area

This nearby natural area eight miles from Bayfield was a place I had never heard about and it was suggested I visit when I stopped at the Visitors Center. This place is a bird lover's dream since it's surrounded by marshy areas. Beaver Hollow offers an abundance of outdoor recreational opportunities such as hiking and snowshoeing in the winter. It is open year round. The parking area is small and there is a kiosk with maps at the entrance. The best thing is the 600 foot accessible boardwalk and crushed gravel walkway. This little-known gem is a quiet place to come and sit in nature.

88850 Compton Road

northpikescreek.org/beaver-hollow

Hiking Trails

Head up the hill on Washington Avenue and you'll find the trailhead to the Gil Larsen Trail, which is just one trail in the Big Ravine Hiking Trails system in Bayfield. This part of the trail is scenic and heavily wooded. Hike the Iron Bridge Loop, which is sometimes a shortcut for Bayfield students heading to school. There are four trailheads that serve Big Ravine Trails.

Another popular trail is the Brownstone Trail that you can catch on 3rd Street and Wilson Avenue. It's an old railroad route that runs along the Lake Superior shoreline.

Downtown Bayfield

Frog Bay Tribal Park

Frog Bay Tribal Park is four miles north of Bayfield and a must-visit. It is the first National Tribal park in the United States. This land is owned by the Red Cliff Band of Lake Superior Chippewa. Inside the park is a nearly two-mile trail through untouched forest and wetlands that leads to the sand beach.

92070 Frog Bay Road

redcliff-nsn.gov/frogbay

Things To Do Near Bayfield

Houghton Falls State Natural Area

Houghton Falls State Natural Area is a short drive south of Bayfield. If time allows, stop here when you leave Washburn on your way north. There is a trail that will take you to the lake. Along the way, you can see the falls. Sometimes it runs dry depending on the rainfall. It's about 3 miles round trip, but worth it. The parking lot is small. Take Highway 13 from Washburn for 2.4 miles, turn right on to Houghton Falls Road.

dnr.wisconsin.gov/topic/statenaturalareas/HoughtonFalls

Shopping

There's plenty of opportunity to spend some cash in Bayfield. Clothing, books, gifts, and outdoor gear are some of the things you can find. Most of the shops are on Rittenhouse Avenue, or on one of the side streets. Bayfield is very much a resort city, so if you are visiting in the off-season, be sure to check if these businesses are open, because most have limited hours or are closed altogether in the winter.

Honest Dog Books

This has to be one of my favorite bookstores on the planet. Honest Dog Books is a cozy, independent bookstore that offers a wide selection of new and used books, as well as gifts and local crafts. It specializes in books about nature, outdoor adventure, and the Northwoods. (Photo page 294)

40 S Second Street

honestdogbooks.com

Apostle Islands Booksellers

Another great bookstore in Bayfield is Apostle Islands Booksellers. It's another independent bookstore that offers a wide selection of books, gifts, and souvenirs. Want to learn more about the area? Apostle Island Booksellers carries books about the Apostle Islands, Lake Superior, and the Northwoods, as well as books from regional authors on local history.

112 Rittenhouse Avenue

apostleislandsbooksellers.com

Howl Downtown

Howl Downtown is a locally owned and operated shop that offers clothing and shoes. It also has a great selection of gifts and souvenirs.

100 Rittenhouse Avenue

howlinbayfield.com

Howl Adventure Center

Howl also has a complete adventure center just outside of Bayfield. Here you will find the gear you need for all your outdoor adventures. E-bikes, outdoor clothing for the whole family, rentals, and more. You can even chill at the bar and enjoy a brew and a taco. Test drive a bike outside on the trail.

35265 S Co Hwy J

howlinbayfield.com

Eckels Pottery & Fine Craft Gallery

Eckels Pottery & Fine Craft Gallery is a family-owned gallery that offers a beautiful selection of handmade pottery, jewelry, and fine crafts. You can watch the potters at work and browse the gallery for unique gifts and souvenirs.

85205 State Highway 13

.eckelspottery.com

Joanne's Scandinavian

Joanne's Scandinavian is a charming gift shop that specializes in Scandinavian imports, including jewelry, textiles, crystal, and more. It also offers a selection of local crafts and gifts.

223 Rittenhouse Avenue

Phone: (715) 779-5772

Stone's Throw

Stone's Throw is a unique shop that offers a variety of gifts, home decor, and clothing, as well as a selection of gourmet foods and beverages. I love its selection of locally made items.

80850 State Highway 13

stonesthrowbayfield.com

stonesthrowbayfield.com/ty HWY J

Silverwaves Jewelry

Silverwaves Jewelry is a beautiful jewelry store that features handmade jewelry made from sterling silver, gemstones, and other materials. You can work with the designers for a beautiful custom piece. Don't you deserve a treat for yourself?

126 Rittenhouse Avenue

silverwaves.nethttps://silverwaves.net/https://silverwaves.net/https://silverwaves.net/

Bayfield Wine and Spirits

Bayfield Wine and Spirits is a specialty wine and liquor store that offers a wide selection of wines, spirits, and craft beers. Stop here and put together a fabulous picnic in the park and watch the boats come in.

13 Second Street

bayfieldwineandspirits.com

Keeper of the Light

Keeper of the Light is a charming gift shop that specializes in Lake Superior and Apostle Island lighthouse-related gifts and souvenirs, including maps, books, and collectibles. It also offers a fun variety of Northwoods-themed items and local crafts.

19 Front Street

keeperofthelight.net

Places To Eat And Drink In Bayfield

Coffee and Bakeries

Wonderstate Coffee

Wonderstate Coffee is a popular coffee shop that has a location in Bayfield and offers a variety of coffee drinks made with sustainably sourced beans from around the world. Grab a pastry or snack and relax at one of the inside tables, or take it to go. Be prepared to stand in line, it's a busy spot!

117 Rittenhouse Avenue

wonderstate.com

Judy's Gourmet Garage

The best homemade pies in the area can be found at this tiny bakery on the way into Bayfield. Get there early, or you might miss some popular items. Gourmet Garage also has other pastries, cheesecakes, cookies and other treats. Only open seasonally and usually Thursday through Sunday.

85130 State Hwy 13

Phone: (715) 779-5365

Restaurants

The Bayfield Inn

The Bayfield Inn is a historic hotel and restaurant that offers a variety of dining options, including a casual pub, a fine dining restaurant, and a rooftop bar with views of Lake Superior. If you have the choice, definitely choose the rooftop bar. The views of Lake Superior and the harbor are stunning. The restaurant specializes in classic American cuisine, with an emphasis on seafood and locally sourced ingredients.

20 Rittenhouse Avenue

bayfieldinn.com

Manypenny Bistro

Manypenny Bistro is a cozy bistro that offers a creative menu featuring locally caught Lake Superior Whitefish, and seasonal ingredients. You'll also find pizza, wraps, sandwiches and burgers. Manypenny Bistro serves breakfast, lunch and dinner.

201 Manypenny Avenue

Phone: (715) 913-0303

Landmark Restaurant in Old Rittenhouse Inn

Rittenhouse Inn is a historic bed and breakfast that also has a fine dining restaurant that offers a gourmet menu featuring fresh, seasonal ingredients. It specializes in multi-course dinners with wine pairings, but also offers a variety of lunch and brunch options. Breakfast here is famous. It's a beautiful setting to enjoy a summer meal. It's open to the public and reservations are recommended.

301 Rittenhouse Avenue

rittenhouseinn.com

The Copper Trout

This upscale family-run restaurant uses fresh local ingredients with Italian flair. Lake Superior Whitefish on pizza? That's what I had and it was fabulous! It's a cozy place to enjoy a wonderful dinner with friends. (Photo page 294)

250 Rittenhouse Avenue

coppertrout.com

Bars, Wineries, and Breweries

Since the wineries in and around Bayfield are part of the Fruit Loop, which was covered in the Highlights section of this chapter, you can find them listed there.

Copper Crow Distillery

Copper Crow Distillery is the first Native American distillery in the United States. It's a craft distillery that produces small-batch spirits, including whiskey, gin, and vodka, using locally sourced grains and botanicals. They have a fun tasting room where the table tops came from a local bowling alley that was dear to the owner's heart, and a canoe hangs from the ceiling. There is also an outdoor seating area where you can sip a specialty drink.

37395 State Highway 13

coppercrowdistillery.com

Accommodations

Hotels and Bed and Breakfast

Bayfield Inn

Bayfield Inn is a waterfront hotel that offers a variety of guest rooms and suites with modern amenities and stunning views of Lake Superior. The Inn also has a restaurant, bar, and coffee shop on-site, as well as a marina.

20 Rittenhouse Avenue

bayfieldinn.com

Legendary Waters Resort & Casino

Legendary Waters Resort & Casino is a Native American-owned resort that features a variety of guest rooms and suites with modern amenities and views of Lake Superior. The resort also has a casino, restaurant, and bar onsite, as well as an indoor pool, hot tub, and fitness center.

37600 Onigamiing Drive, Red Cliff

legendarywaters.com

Artesian House Bed and Breakfast

Artesian House Bed and Breakfast is a cozy eco-friendly inn that offers comfortable guest rooms with private baths and modern amenities. Owners Christine and Dennis also offer a spectacular complimentary breakfast with locally made bakery items. There's access to a shared living room and outdoor patio. A bonus for guests: Christine and Dennis are welcoming hosts with a wealth of knowledge about the area. For this reason, it's my pick when I stay in the area.

84100 Hatchery Road

artesianhouse.com

Pinehurst Inn

Pinehurst Inn is an eco-friendly bed and breakfast that features eight comfortable guest rooms with private baths, modern amenities, and access to a sauna and outdoor hot tub. Guests also are treated to a gourmet breakfast made with locally sourced ingredients, as well as afternoon tea and homemade treats.

83645 State Highway 13

pinehurstinn.com

Old Rittenhouse Inn

Old Rittenhouse Inn is a historic bed and breakfast that features elegant guest rooms with antique furnishings, private baths, and modern amenities. The inn and grounds sit high overlooking Rittenhouse Avenue, and Lake Superior. It's a fabulous Instagram-worthy shot, especially in summer when the flowers are in bloom.

301 Rittenhouse Avenue

rittenhouseinn.com

Campgrounds

Apostle Islands Area Campground

Apostle Islands Area Campground is a family-friendly campground that offers tent and RV sites with full hookups and some drive through sites, as well as cabins and a real covered wagon! There's a variety of amenities, including a swimming pool, playground, basketball court, and a camp store.

85150 Trailer Court Road

aiacamping.com

SUPERIOR

NESTLED AT THE WESTERN tip of the Great Lake Superior, Superior, Wisconsin, is a picturesque harbor town brimming with history, vibrant culture, and natural beauty. The town holds a strategic place in American history because of its prime location as a shipping port. Its historical roots delve deep into Native American history, the fur trading epoch, and the early industrial period. Today, Superior is not just a testament to its splendid past, but also a dynamic hub of activities, attractions, and culinary delights.

Location

Superior is the northernmost Wisconsin Harbor Town, roughly 80 miles from Bayfield. You'll definitely want to take scenic Highway 13 if you are coming directly from Bayfield. It skims the Lake Superior shoreline.

Superior Facts

- The region that would become Superior was originally inhabited by Native American tribes, including the Ojibwe. The area was rich in fur-bearing animals, attracting European fur traders and explorers in the 17th century.

- Superior was formally established in the mid-19th century, spurred by its strategic location on Lake Superior and the booming logging industry. It quickly grew as a transportation and shipping hub because of its proximity to valuable natural resources.

- The late 19th and early 20th centuries saw Superior experiencing significant economic growth, largely driven by its thriving port, which facilitated the trade of goods like lumber, coal, and grain. The mid-20th century brought economic challenges, including the decline of traditional industries. However, investments in education, tourism, and new industries helped in reviving the town's economy in the latter part of the century. Today, Superior is a vibrant harbor town known for its rich history, recreational opportunities, diverse culinary scene, and as a gateway to the natural beauty of the surrounding regions, balancing its historical heritage with modern.

- Superior has a population of 26,561 (2021)

How Much Time To Spend In Superior

Superior is worthy of at least a weekend to explore the city, perhaps a day or two more if you'd like to visit Duluth, Minnesota. I definitely recommend spending some time at Canal Park in Duluth.

Things To Do In Superior

Superior Highlights

Lighthouse

Superior Entry Lighthouse - Resting at the end of Wisconsin Point, the Superior Entry Lighthouse began its service in 1913. Its 2-story oval shape and tower is a favorite of photographers. The lighthouse was automated in 1970 and is on the National Register of Historic Places. The lighthouse was put up for auction in 2019 and the winning bidder was a tech executive from San Francisco, who purchased it for $159,000. At this time, it is not open to the public but you can view it by boat.

SS Meteor Whaleback Ship Museum

Superior is home to the last remaining whaleback ship, the SS Meteor. The whaleback ship was the brainchild of Captain Alexander McDougall. This new design featured a flatter bottom for more cargo space and a tipped up bow. The new style vessel was called a "whaleback" and was first launched in 1888. The Meteor was launched in 1896 from the shipyard of McDougall's company, American Steel Barge Company. Today the site of that company is known as Frasher Shipyards.

There is a fee for the museum and tour with a reduced rate for seniors, kids, and active military. Please note that the ship has multiple ladders and stairs to climb. They advise wearing closed-toe shoes with a good grip and no skirts or dresses. (Photo page 294)

200 Marina Drive

superiorpublicmuseums.org/ss-meteor

Fairlawn Mansion & Museum

Fairlawn Mansion served as the original home of logging baron Martin Pattison, his wife Grace, and their six children. Built in 1889 and completed the following year, Fairlawn encompasses 42 rooms in 15,000 square feet. The opulent Victorian mansion offers a glimpse into the life of Superior's past elite, showcasing stunning architecture and historical exhibits.

I would suggest taking a tour of the mansion to learn the history behind the family and the mansion's later service as the Superior Children's Home And Refuge.

906 East 2nd. Street

superiorpublicmuseums.org/fairlawn-mansion

Richard I. Bong Veterans Historical Center

Dedicated to honoring veterans, this museum provides insightful exhibits on U.S military history, focusing on the life and career of Major Richard I. Bong, a decorated US Army Air Force pilot during World War II. It is well worth a visit just to learn about this local hero. The staff is so knowledgeable, friendly, and willing to tell the stories about our wars and the veterans who fought for our freedoms - important stories to pass down to future generations.

305 East 2nd Street

bongcenter.org

Wisconsin Point

Offering more than 200 acres of land, Wisconsin Point is an ideal location for birdwatching, hiking, and enjoying serene beach activities. It's also rich in indigenous history and is a significant part of the Lake Superior Water Trail.

.ci.superior.wi.us/226/Wisconsin-Point

Barkers Island

You may not know it from seeing it, but Barkers Island is a man-made island. It's made from the material dredged from the harbor to create the deep shipping lanes needed for large ships. Today, Barkers Island is a place to visit with a swimming beach, a resort, trails, a marina and home to the Meteor Whaleback Ship.

Pattison State Park

Even though it's located a bit out of Superior, Pattison State Park is a must-see. Pattison State Park is a remarkable natural retreat, celebrated for its breathtaking scenery and diverse outdoor activities. The park's crowning glory is Big Manitou Falls, the highest waterfall in Wisconsin, cascading majestically at 165 feet. Complementing this natural wonder is the serene Little Manitou Falls, standing at 30 feet. These falls not only provide stunning visual backdrops but also make for excellent spots for nature photography.

The park boasts a network of hiking trails that cater to various skill levels, each trail offering unique views of the waterfalls and the dense forest surrounding them. These trails are popular among nature lovers and offer an immersive experience in the park's lush landscape.

For visitors seeking a more leisurely experience, Pattison State Park has well-equipped picnic areas, complete with tables and grills, ideal for family outings or a peaceful day in the great outdoors. During the warmer months, the park's beach area becomes a hub of activity, with visitors enjoying swimming and sunbathing. Those wishing to extend their visit have the option of camping, as the park provides facilities for both tents and RVs. This allows for a more in-depth exploration of the park and its natural beauty.

When winter sets in, the park transforms into a haven for snowshoeing and cross-country skiing, with trails specially maintained for these winter activities. This seasonal shift in the park's landscape provides a unique experience for visitors.

Entry requires either a day pass or a Wisconsin State Park sticker.

6294 WI Hwy 35

wisconsin.gov/topic/parks/pattison

Shopping

Superior is excellent for thrift and antique shopping. You will also find a great mix of clothing and gift shops. Most shops are on Tower Avenue and Belknap Streets, making it easy to spend a half day there. You can easily walk, but if you have mobility issues, you may need to park your car, stop in a few shops, and drive to the next spot. Parking is easy and free. These are some of my favorites:

Sweden Sweets

Looking to satisfy your sweet tooth? This is a candy mecca. Fudge, taffy, old-fashioned candy, popcorn, it's all here. There is a soda fountain style counter where you can get ice cream. It's so much fun to stop in here. Even if you don't plan to buy anything, I can tell you that you will find a candy that brings you back to your childhood.

601 Tower Avenue

sweedensweets.com

Angie's Closet

This women's consignment store is full of fabulous brand name fashions at reasonable prices. They cater to everyone and are size inclusive. For someone like myself who loves giving new life to a discarded piece of clothing, it's a must stop.

1315 Tower Avenue

angiesclosetresale.com

Earth Exchange

This is a huge two-level thrift store, so it takes some time to browse. The concept of the store is to serve a purpose in the community with the offering of new and used furniture and new mattresses at deeply discounted prices. Furniture is not the only thing you will find here. There is a mix of clothing for the whole family, home decor and other items. Earth Exchange was founded on the premise of doing something positive for the environment.

1713 Belknap Street

earthexchange.org

Globe News

If you are a gamer, vinyl collector, and/or a sports card collector, stop in at Globe News. The store also hosts game nights and other events. It's a cool store in a historical building. You can't

miss its location on the corner of Tower Avenue and Belknap Street.

1430 Tower Avenue

Phone: (715) 392-2090

Places To Eat And Drink In Superior

Coffee and Bakery

Empire Coffee

This coffee shop is a popular spot for locals and visitors. They offer premium coffee from local vendors and a fabulous sandwich menu. Empire Coffee is a welcoming, cozy place to enjoy a cuppa and either visit with friends or get some work done.

1204 Tower Avenue

empirecoffeewi.com

Restaurants

Superior Family Restaurant

How can you not love the down-hominess of a local family restaurant? In Superior, that place is the Superior Family Restaurant. You can find it in the historic Androy Hotel, which was built in 1925. You will find all the staples here. It has a full all-day breakfast menu, along with lunch and dinner options.

1213 Tower Avenue

superiorfamilyrestaurant.com

Anchor Bar

Anchor Bar is famous for two things. Their burgers and fries (the only menu items) and its claim to fame for being on the Food Network television show 'Diners, Drive-Ins and Dives'. The bar is really cool, dark and full of memorabilia. It's a popular place, so I would suggest going early. It has become a tourist destination and a place to hang out for locals, as well as the crew members who arrive in port from big ships. Try the Olive Burger!

413 Tower Avenue

anchorbarandgrill.com

Gronk's Grill and Bar

If you aren't noticing a theme here, there are many fantastic eating places inside well-established bars in Superior. Gronk's is one of them. It's home to the one pound Mighty Mammoth Burger and the Upside Down Burger. You can also enjoy pizza, chicken, and daily specials.

4909 East 2nd Street

gronksgrill.com

Guadalajara Mexican Restaurant

Best place in town for Mexican food at excellent prices. All your favorites and I love the colorful and lively atmosphere. There is also the Arcade Bar where you can enjoy drinks and play arcade games.

69 North 28th Street

superiorwimexicanrestaurant.com

Bars, Wineries, and Breweries

Cedar Lounge Earth Rider Brewery

If you want to taste the local Earth Rider brews from next door, Cedar Lounge is the official tasting room. The bartenders are super knowledgeable and can answer all your beer questions. Pub food is served here, which includes our favorite item, Ashland Baking Company pretzels. Cedar Lounge has live music and game nights. I recommend the Blueberry Honey cream ale.

1617 North 3rd. Street

earthrider.beer

Accommodations

Hotels

There are many hotel chains that serve the Superior area.

Androy Hotel

This is a historical Neoclassical hotel, built in 1925 and known as the "million dollar hotel". It was once occupied by then senator John F. Kennedy in 1960 when he was in town for a reception at the hotel. Today the hotel, which has undergone renovations, is still a nod to the simplistic opulence of the day. It may not be the Ritz, but is pretty cool to step inside.

1213 Tower Avenue

androyhotel.com

Barkers Island Inn and Conference Center

Basic accommodations on Barkers Island near the marina. 111 rooms with a pool area, lounge, and restaurant. The inn has easy access to downtown Superior.

300 Marina Drive

barkersislandinn.com

Campgrounds

Pattison State Park

There are 59 campsites in the park, with 18 of them electric sites. What I love about this campground is its sites are wooded, so they are private, even though some are close together. Most sites are drive through, which is nice. There is a beach area and hiking trails. Pattison is home to Big Manitou Falls, Wisconsin's biggest waterfall.

6294 WI Hwy 35

dnr.wisconsin.gov/topic/parks/pattison

PHOTO REFERENCE

Front Cover Photo-Bayfield Pier

Page 74 Photos

Mader's -Milwaukee

Kenosha Public Museum-Kenosha

The Chocolate Chisel-Port Washington

Kayaking The River-Milwaukee

Bronze Fonz-Milwaukee

Wind Point Lighthouse-Racine

Best Place At Historic Pabst Brewery-Milwaukee

Page 123 Photos

Cedar Crest Ice Cream Parlor-Manitowoc

Lottie Cooper-Sheboygan

John Michael Kohler Art Preserve-Sheboygan

Cool City Brewing-Two Rivers

Kohler Andrae State Park-Sheboygan

Hamilton Wood Type & Printing Museum-Two Rivers

Sly's Midtown Saloon-Sheboygan

Page 180 Photos

Island Orchard Cider-Door County

Cave Point Kayak Tour-Door County

Mural-Algoma

Sister Golden-Door County

View From Stone Harbor Resort-Sturgeon Bay

Page 241 Photos

Beyer Home-Oconto

Copper State Brewing Co.-Green Bay

Packers Heritage Trail-Green Bay

Menekaunee Harbor and Park-Marinette

The Shop On Main-Oconto

Page 294 Photos

Honest Dog Books-Bayfield

The Copper Trout-Bayfield

Mural-Ashland

PHOTO REFERENCE

Maslowski Beach Park-Ashland

SS Meteor Whaleback Ship-Superior

ABOUT THE AUTHOR

Lori Helke is a travel writer and the creator of the "Lori Loves Adventure" blog, designed to inspire midlife women with enriching solo travel tips and experiences.

She is the author of the children's book series "Beatrice The Little Camper" and her first travel guide *Wisconsin Harbor Towns: The Ultimate Charming Wisconsin Road Trip Guide*. Besides her literary pursuits, Lori contributes to a monthly travel segment on a local morning television show and has contributed to several print and online publications. She lives in Wisconsin with her husband, Rick, and rescue dog Vivi.

Travel Blog: lorilovesadventure.com

Author Site: lorihelke.com

www.ingramcontent.com/pod-product-compliance
Lightning Source LLC
Chambersburg PA
CBHW072148070526
44585CB00015B/1049